Managing Millennials

Managing Millennials

Shaping a New Work Paradigm

Jacqueline Cripps

BEP

BUSINESS EXPERT PRESS

Leader in applied, concise business books

Managing Millennials: Shaping a New Work Paradigm

Copyright © Business Expert Press, LLC, 2024

Cover design by Anis El Idrissi

Interior design by Exeter Premedia Services Private Ltd., Chennai, India

First published in 2023 by
Business Expert Press, LLC
222 East 46th Street, New York, NY 10017
www.businessexpertpress.com

ISBN-13: 978-1-63742-512-1 (paperback)
ISBN-13: 978-1-63742-513-8 (e-book)

Business Expert Press Human Resource Management and
Organizational Behavior Collection

First edition: 2023

10 9 8 7 6 5 4 3 2 1

Description

Leadership. Engagement. Retention. Recruitment. Diversity. The key challenges facing workplaces today.

Underpinning these challenges is the millennial workforce:

- A generation who are experiencing global challenges like the economic crisis, debt, job insecurity, and housing unaffordability.
- A generation who are experiencing personal challenges like social media addictions, pressure, and mental health crisis.
- A generation who has been put in the "too hard" basket by a lot of workplaces.
- A generation who are soon to become the dominant global workforce.

To future-proof workplace performance and engagement, workplaces must act.

Getting the best out of the millennial workforce means creating an environment where they can thrive. Critical to this is good management and leadership. Without it, workplaces will not resolve the current challenges.

This book provides a solution. It's designed to educate readers on the current and future millennial workforce: who they are, what they want, what they need, and how to get the best out of them. It offers clear-cut guidance and best practice techniques for both managers and millennials as they continue to navigate the current and future landscape of work.

Keywords

managing millennials; managing workforce; leadership development

Contents

Introduction

I'm going to start with a story. Not because this book isn't one big story (loosely defined, of course) but because, in simple terms, it outlines one of the reasons why I'm writing this book.

As I'm writing this in the comfort of my home office, it's June 2022, and an uncharacteristic warm day for England. In fact, so much so that "experts" have put out a newsworthy heat warning (because let's face it, anything over a mere 25 degrees centigrade in this country is unpalatable). A contrast, dare I say to last week, where I found myself seated around a table of Executives discussing organizational strategy, in blistery Glasgow.

It wasn't so much the weather that was the problem, but the situation I found myself in, which took me back to a time before I'd started this journey of becoming a leader in my field, and what I continue will be, a voice for millennials. A time where I'd suddenly regressed to my 21-year-old self: a fresh graduate stepping into the workplace for the first time and being met firmly with resistance and contrast. Both within myself (being the "new person" in a foreign environment, with foreign people, weighed with the feeling of being under the spotlight and a desperate need to do or say something of value) and from those around me (also being that "new person" who is also "young" and "knows nothing" about how things are done and presents as a threat to older colleagues who are less receptive to fresh faced talent). No one likes being the new person in any situation, let alone carrying that weight of baggage and stepping into the fray of an unknown workplace.

I digress.

Back to the story, there were several things that I was struck by:

- The demographics of the Executives, who were all of Boomer generation or older.
- Their body language, which was for lack of a better word, exclusively closed off.

- The position of where I was seated for the first half of the day (in the corner of the room alongside another external guest).
- The position of where I was seated for the second half of the day (in a small space that was accommodated for a few shuffled papers and tight smiles, which if I hadn't requested, would have remained seated in the corner).
- A seemingly unwillingness to listen to my contribution, not just demonstrated through a lack of asking my thoughts or input, but when I finally created a space to offer my voice, was met with polite smiles and "next steps" on the agenda.
- My own feelings: a general sense of not belonging, not being accepted, and not being respected as a colleague.
- The then internal questioning and chastising: Did I do something wrong? Did I say something offensive? Should I have stayed in the corner? Was I too assertive? Followed quickly by the feeling of frustration that this dynamic—how I was being treated—was not something I would tolerate (including thoughts on my "exit speech" and reasons why I wasn't going to be part of this "toxicity").
- Serious reassessment of whether I would continue my working relationship with the organization. Before finally, the light bulb of the "ah ha!" moment of what was happening in the room (admittedly accompanied by stupidity): Intergenerational conflict. The very thing I teach!

A humbling situation that demonstrated (for me) that no matter how aware we are, there are moments—and especially being a millennial with a driving desire to not just add value but be respected and treated as an equal—that we are easily influenced by those we work with. And it made me wonder that if I had suddenly fallen victim to it—even with the awareness of what was going on and knowing what I do about the complications of the workplace—then I can only assume there are countless numbers of other millennials who are too.

And that's where the issue is.

This book is as much about teaching millennials how to understand and manage themselves, as much as it is teaching managers and those

Executives how we want to be treated to get the best out of us. And while there are many stereotypes out there that have, in some parts, unhelpfully defined our generation, for those millennial leaders and workplaces who want to nurture their leaders, there is huge potential. Potential that I believe, we are still, only scratching the surface of.

CHAPTER 1

Being Millennial

Values, Traits, and Skills

The Challenge

Millennials are, and continue to be, a misjudged and misunderstood generation. And while we are moving into a new age of understanding, there are ways to go before this generation and those around are in a place of comfort. These misperceptions and lack of understanding present an imminent challenge for workplaces—as our up-and-coming global workforce and those leading are millennials. This trajectory of growth which statistics indicate is as high as 75 percent by 2025, means that it's happening *regardless* of the world and workplaces being ready.

Millennials are both the future workforce and future leaders. While theoretically this might not look problematic per se, the complexities and interdependencies between these situations must be understood. More paramount, however, is the need to resolve any disconnect between (1) the absence of understanding by workplaces of who and what millennials are and (2) the need for millennials to better understand themselves as people and leaders in the context of their workplace and the wider world.

Millennials have qualities and traits that have potential to bring huge growth to any workplace. However, there are still vast amounts of untapped potential within organizations that is failing to be used and, if explored, has the power to change both the individual themselves and the workplace. The challenge that workplaces are experiencing, however, isn't just about this "unknown potential," but how to tap into it.

There is a known issue—for both millennials and their respective colleagues—of the absence of understanding. For decades, millennials have adopted the label of being a generation of challenges. The misunderstood aspect is notable to those other generations who, in the context of their lives, have not been able to relate to this "new" generation in the workplace. One doesn't need to go far to see/hear/taste/smell the preconceived notions, expectations, ideals (or lack of), and stereotypes—"lazy," "self-entitled," and "unfocused"—that tend to find their way toward millennials.

What has been occurring at the same time, often operating in the background, is the dual complexity: the generation not truly understanding themselves. (We only need to look at the mental health stats.) And while this generation is resilient, especially in the face of change, the "thick-skinned" approach which they've adopted (against the "snowflake" perception) is wearing thin as the world continues to offer challenges. The internalization underneath the façade—who am I, what should I do, and how to get by—is eating them alive and adding to the complexity of unknowns.

Whatever side of the misunderstood coin should be flipped, right now we have two complex situations: the latter—at least demonstrated by stats—perhaps the highest risk. This inability of millennials to understand themselves means they are unable to identify and articulate what they want or need in life. And in turn, educate and create awareness toward those people, places, or institutions that influence a large part (if not all) of their lives.

This ignorance is widespread. The language being spoken between millennials, workplaces, and institutions in the world isn't aligned. Alarmingly creating an environment that provides a backdrop for blame and disconnection continues to occur in society. And what we're seeing is ongoing problems and ripple effect impacts. Band-aid solutions, reactive responses, temporary answers—none of which are providing sustainable solutions because getting to the root of the matter—the heart—isn't occurring (at least not to the level that requires sustainable change).

How this plays out socially—and institutionally—is yet to be seen or experienced to the gravity, but several possibilities exist. For government, the potential for greater dependencies on handouts, with the cost of living at all-time high, was exacerbated by the recession and inflation. For higher education institutions (universities and colleges), reduction in student numbers and inability to attract talent—resulting in reduced income and a critical need to re-examine course curriculums, academic workloads, fee structures, and teaching methods. For health care, greater strain on mental health services and public health system as rates of anxiety and depression increase. For financial institutions, accumulation of debt and the need to examine alternative ways to provide accessible and affordable funding solutions that absorb rising interest rates. For corporations, pressure to examine global and sustainability priorities and commitments and ensure ethics and sustainability are at the core of products and services.

Finally, for workplaces and businesses, pressures for changes in ways of working and the need to future-proof success via solid leadership and management—leveraging the skills and talent of those who are already (or almost) at the driver's seat: millennial managers and the future Executive C-Suite.

The Why

Millennials make up approximately 1.8 billion of the global population.[1] And arguably, they have been anointed with being a "generation of challenges." Social, economic, political, or historical, whatever the event past, present, or future, has shaped and will continue to shape who this generation is. What this means for workplaces is that the millennial experience is complex. Not just because of the values, traits, and skills but because of their conditioned experience and worldview—which includes the current environment. And part of the challenge that workplaces feel—the frustration with not understanding or relating—has to do with this.

Which means the solution lies in the problem. That being, the whole of millennials and what they bring must be understood in the context of their complex experience. Complexity by way of values, needs, and wants; and the necessity to unpick all of this in a way that is clear, aligned, and understood.

Management Best Practices

What Millennials Want

Comparative to their situation and lives, what millennials want from there managers is simple: to be recognized, heard, and understood. Learning their language—who they are (values), how they've come to be who they are (environment), and what they want to achieve—is core to that.

---

[1] United Nations, Department of Economic and Social Affairs, Population Division. 2019. *World Population Prospects 2019: Highlights* (ST/ESA/SER.A/423).

While generations and generational-specific challenges will be explored in Chapter 2, understanding the basics—including key events that have shaped this generation—is a must. It offers a platform for demonstrating how the events which have transpired over the decades, and the consequences, have influenced their current lives, such as:

- Family—Increased parental emphasis on child rearing (i.e., helicopter parenting) (1980s to present)
- Socially—Computers and technology (including the Y2K) and the rise of social media (1990s to present); increased activism and social protesting (e.g., the MeToo movement, gender, and sexuality beliefs)
- Politically—September 11, 2001 (2000s)
- Economically—The 2008 Recession (Global Financial Crisis and Recession) and the 2019 pandemic (and subsequent recession) (2000s; 2010s to present)
- Environment—Climate change and global warming recognitions, new approaches to diversity and inclusion (2010s to present)

It is these key events that have shaped the generation and who they have become.

How millennials were raised has arguably been one of the most influential factors affecting the generation. The "excessive involvement" approach has created a culture programmed for reward, achievement, expectations, and arguably an unrealistic view (and mismatch) of "how the real world" works.

The late 1990s saw the rise of technology and its newfound importance in our lives. However, it didn't come without uncertainty—bringing with it a duality of benefit and risk. Powerful advances and recognition of our future dependency countered with fear that it could end the world (Y2K of 1999). It was arguably one of the first global problems that millennials encountered.

The rise in social media beginning in the 2000s has been hugely defining: offering freedom of thought, speech, and global connection. The off-set, however, over the preceding decades has brought about dependencies, instant gratification syndrome, technology addictions (vis-à-vis market-ing algorithms), comparison mentality, and bullying rise. In turn, leading to well-being challenges with emotional and mental health: self-esteem, self-worth, inadequacy, and feelings of failure. Furthermore, the conse-quences of overparenting have presented a background hum of pressure, with ideals and expectations around career choices and life milestones carved out for them.

The decade of 2000 brought a defining historical moment, with the September 11 attacks on the World Trade Center. The ripple effect of eco-nomic challenges around the world, including the Global Financial Crisis of 2008, saw (and continues to see) millennials accumulate the highest levels of student loan debt, poverty, unemployment, and lower levels of wealth and personal income than any other comparative generation. The continuation of global inflation, the rising cost of living, and housing unaffordability have all led to ongoing financial challenges and debt cri-ses. Progressively, this generation has also been pivotal in witnessing and advocating change: the election of Barack Obama in 2008, a defining moment that reflected social progress; and the same-sex marriage rights recognition (the United States) in 2015.

Currently, the effects of the pandemic are being felt—including the political, economic, and social instability—which have exacerbated these issues. And in turn, contributing most profoundly to mental health issues: rising rates of anxiety, stress, depression, eating disorders, and addictions.[2]

[2] M. McCreary. 2015. *Anxiety and Work: The Impact of Anxiety on Different Gener-ations of Employees* (U.S.: Morneau Shepell); D. Gruttadaro and D. Crudo. 2012. *College Students Speak: A Survey Report on Mental Health* (U.S.: The National Alliance on Mental Illness); G. Henriques. 2014. "The College Student Mental Health Crisis Today's College Students Are Suffering From an Epidemic of Men-tal Illnesses," *Psychology Today.* www.psychologytoday.com; The National Eating Disorders Association. 2018. *Statistics and Research on Eating Disorders.* www .nationaleatingdisorders.org; J.R. Knight, H. Weschler, M. Kuo, M. Seibring, E.R. Weitzman, and M.A. Schuckit. 2015. "Alcohol Abuse and Depend-ence Among U.S. College Students," *Journal of Studies on Alcohol* 63, no. 3, pp. 263–270; T. Curran and P.H. Andrew. 2019. "Perfectionism Is Increasing Over Time: A Meta-Analysis of Birth Cohort Differences From 1989 to 2016," *Psychological Bulletin* 145, no. 4, pp. 410–429.

While the events of the last decades have been hugely influential—and left lasting impacts on this generation—the solution isn't to be found in changing history. Rather, understanding. And this generational level of understanding is the first step.

What does this mean for the workplace? The short answer, and where the biggest impacts are being felt, is to do with values mismatch: misalignment and/or misunderstanding of workplaces on what matters to millennials and why. And it's for this reason that the ripple effects of behavior and attitudes that play out in the office—for example, requesting higher salaries because they need to pay off debts, freely expressing their thoughts and ideas without hesitation, demanding more accountability or transparency, or productivity- and performance-related issues due to mental health stressors—which is causing friction.

Pleased to Meet You: Millennial Values

Acknowledgment and acceptance of values are key. But what does one mean when we talk about values? Is this another "whishy washy demand" of this generation? The answer is no—and arguably for managers, the most important thing to learn about this generation (alongside their personal stories). That being, what matters to them, what they find important, and then how that translates into their day to day.

It's perhaps easiest to think of values as a north star—what drives motivation and behavior. While in some cases, millennials might not themselves readily know how to articulate what this values framework is for them, it will (consciously or not) determine their actions, behavior, and decisions. While acknowledging that yes, individual differences, preferences, and personalities do play a role and will offer individual contrast to varying degrees, there are core values that are consistent with this generation—irrespective of the changes going on in the world.

How to Support

Getting the best out of your millennials means listening: recognizing needs, appreciating wants, and building an environment that supports that. The core to this is understanding how millennials are hardwired and driven—through their values and, in turn, how this translates into skills, traits, and behavior. Doing it well will equip managers with new avenues of leverage and management and the increased chances of driving performance and engagement. And alongside that, an increase in loyalty through demonstrating one of the things this generation wants most of all: to be heard. Not listed in any order, the following key values are at the heart of the millennial make up.

Authenticity

Millennials speak from the heart, from what they know. They aren't afraid to offer an opinion when they feel it's warranted. Not from a know-it-all point but from an I-like-to-be-heard point of view. While often misunderstood by many generations as being "disrespectful" or "rude," millennials simply operate from a place of authenticity (albeit there are occasions where they could demonstrate a little more tact with their expression). And while begrudgingly for some managers, it triggers irritation, there is much to be said about the fresh perspective that challenges (respectively) this "keep the peace" approach, instead replacing it with a "why" or "tell me more." For managers, **providing a supportive environment in the workplace matters**. Being able to show up as themselves, without concerns about how they'll be perceived, or accepted, means millennials bring their whole selves to work, and, in turn, workplaces can get the most out of them.

Individuality

Millennials are idiosyncratic people—not necessarily in the quirky or peculiar sense, more that they have a disposition that is unique. This is the contrast most see playing out against other generations: a new viewpoint, a new lens, a dissatisfaction for the status quo, and a want to do things different, all because they want to be better, do better, and fundamentally make their lives and the planet a better place. For managers, **celebrating individuality and making space for innovation matters**. Millennials are then able to offer new ideas, innovative concepts, and how to do things more effectively.

Open-Minded

Not to be confused with a "laisse fair" attitude, millennials are open-minded and adopt broad mentalities—complimenting in part other values that lie around diversity. All of which go hand in hand with the desire for prosocial change—something which drives millennials forward. We only need to reflect on the progressive changes that have occurred in recent years, supported by a generation who has equality, diversity, and inclusion (EDI) at heart; millennial activism, if you will. For managers, **providing a safe space and offering a platform where conversations and issues that matter can be discussed in a fair, equitable, and respectful way matters.** Doing so will both encourage and allow millennials to share their voice on all matters of EDI and offer an opportunity for being ambassadors for causes that matter.

Flexible

A core attribute, and perhaps becoming increasingly demanded of in this postpandemic world, is flexibility. Millennials are a generation who are flexible and open to change. This fluidity isn't just from a thoughts and beliefs perspective but in the very way they live life. They aren't designed as "creatures of habit" but more about embracing the colors and variations that life has to offer. This means you won't see them sitting on the sidelines watching from afar but rather rolling up their sleeves and diving in. And regardless of the conditions, this generation will move through life with a willingness to make things happen—as if a mission. For managers, **providing flexibility in the when, where, and how millennials do their work matters.** With change a steady constant in their lives, millennials are readily able to adjust to changing environments that include ways of working, making them key leaders for supporting postpandemic operations and environments.

Adaptable

Operating from an intuitive, natural, purpose-driven place of being, millennials are highly adaptable. Millennials like to add value by offering taste and perspective vis-à-vis the interactions they have over the world.

Leaving an essence of what they want and what they hope will be a legacy: for something important, impactful, and change-making because they want to leave the world in a better place. This is also why they are considered "people of change": focused on the greater good, they seek careers that have meaning, careers that have a purpose, careers that won't just change their lives but that of others because social responsibility and contribution matter. For managers, **allowing millennials space to lead and invoke change matters.** Millennials can shift and adapt to change easier than other generations—and in some respects, advocate for how to do things better, whether that be process, ways of working, or simply being.

Freedom and Autonomy

Millennials are independent, yet team players; dual components that complement. However, they want to control their own lives—despite societal pressures. They typically don't like being told what to do—which isn't due to lack of respect, simply because they like to figure things out themselves. Millennials have their own point of view and coupled with a solution-oriented mindset, they enjoy experimenting, creating, and coming up with solutions. For managers, **encouraging autonomy and creative freedom matters.** Allowing freedom offers millennials space to present ideas, use their innovative mindsets, and outside-of-the-box mentality—all of which can be used to the advantage of workplaces.

Technology

As a generation of digital natives, millennials place huge value in technology. Not just because it's a tool to make life easier, more efficient, and convenient, but it's a revolutionized way of connecting with the world. Coupled with an appetite and thirst for "all things new," including the exploration of culture and experience, millennials have been able to navigate the technology and social media "systems" to their advantage. For managers, **allowing millennials to use technology and/or ensuring that platforms exist that support their willingness to bring efficiencies into their day to day matter.** Encouraging the use of technology to get things done faster and more efficiently provides huge workplace advantages through cost and efficiency reductions and savings (time, effort, and money).

Learning

Millennials are hardworking and productive; they are motivated to achieve. They want to learn. Active feedback, encouragement, and support are something they want and critical to engagement—not just in the workplace but in all areas of life. For they are a generation who are conditioned for rewards and stimulation. For managers, **supporting the development of goals matters.** Millennials will strive for any meaningful goals—the prize as simple as the achievement of it. And the more engaged they are in their pursuits, the more workplaces will get in return.

"I hear you," "I see you," "Let me help you," "I respect you," "I value you," "Thank you." Behind all of this is a want that millennials have, to feel valued. Part of the role—and challenge—that managers have, is to find the way to do this, which is easy. And the simplest way is to discover who they are at the core. While this may take time, like any relationship, the first part managers can do is to make a commitment to get to know your millennials in a way that is meaningful to them. To create a place that they feel they can show up as their whole selves and put everything they have into what they do, so they can be the best versions they can be, both for you and themselves.

For Millennials: How to Get What You Want

It's not about you, but it is about you—which means to get what you want and need requires a look at.

As a generation, there are things that we know; those "truths" (for us) which we see happening. We know the world feels complicated and complex: mixed messages, pressures, societal expectations and ideals, changes fluctuating with the world economy, politics, health, poverty—you name it. We know there is a range of dynamic factors churning around, creating a whirlwind of uncertainty and instability. And we also know the stigma, labels, and assumptions that are made about our generation—and the challenge of feeling unheard, misunderstood, or unacknowledged. It's life—and for our generation, knowing about the things around us should make it easier to navigate. However, to move forward and start bringing into reality the things we want require an equal contribution on our part, to show up and do the work.

The purpose of highlighting the societal, political, and economic influences (and challenges) that we have (and are) still experiencing isn't to offer justification, or worse, a platform for victimhood. It's the opposite. The irony, however, is **despite the issues our generation is facing, the level of awareness among us isn't where it could (or should) be.** This means we end up feeling alone in our battles because we don't understand the context that sits around our generation—especially the factors that predispose us to the experiences we are now having.

When we start adopting a broader mindset, we can see it's not a one-size-fits-all model, and multiple causes exist. Causes that are relevant to our generation—and in some parts, "normal." Meaning that the challenges we face are validated. This doesn't give us a free pass to do nothing, we must act; and with an informed outlook and educated stance, we can make better decisions that support us and others. By taking control, vis-à-vis our awareness and knowledge, we are elevated to a position of power to make choices and decisions.

Like most problems, when we know what we are dealing with, we are in a better position to start working on the solution. While we cannot control external factors, we can choose how we respond. Meaning with the right support, we can shift our lens and perspective and start taking control. We don't know what we don't know—which means for us to be able to articulate what we want in a way that translates to those listening means, we need to understand the basics of us. And these basics lie in understanding our generation and what makes us "us." How we've been raised, what we've experienced, and how this has shaped our values—providing a canvas for our lives and informing our wants, needs, thoughts, feelings, and behavior.

So, with that said, **how do we help our workplaces understand "what it means to be millennial?" How do we articulate ourselves in a way where we feel heard, recognized, and understood?**

Understand Who You Are and What You Want.   This includes what you want and need from your managers to be the best version of yourself. And if you need to take time to work that out—research, reflect, or plan— do that. Being unprepared and unclear will only work against you.

Remove Any Blame or Victim Mentality.   There is no guide to understanding any generation, and millennials are no exception, so pointing the finger isn't going to help. Nor is complaining about things we're missing or lacking. Our voice and authenticity are our power—which means that turning it on ourselves and being ready to show up for ourselves and have progressive, respectful conversations is what we must do.

Identify Where You Can Add Value.   There are countless ways millennials can add value to a workplace, so get clear on how you can do that. It's not up to your managers—although their support does help. Not only does it offer the approach of "how can I help" or "how can I be of service" (which is our mentality and what we value: to be of value, create impact, and make a difference), but it creates a space of reciprocity and respect.

Shift Perspective.   Recognize that your managers aren't looking at life through the same lens as you. If they are an older demographic, respect who they are, and drawing on your understanding of generations, appreciate their alternative lens on life. If they're a fellow millennial, then talk to them as you would yourself. The dialect between millennials already exists, providing one less translation barrier to exist.

Have a Conversation.   There shouldn't be any reason why having a conversation in real time isn't possible. Face to face, virtual, or phone call. There is a tendency for our generation to easily sit behind a computer screen, with some experiencing discomfort with phone calls. But the risk of only communicating via technology is the loss in translation aspect— which, for the sake of getting what we desire, must be avoided.

This also means understanding the "what we mean" versus "what is heard" doesn't always align. Especially over platforms that lack social cues and body language (hello, e-mail, and text). Be mindful of barriers and context. Sure, warm your managers up and be expressive but try to have a human connection. Be open about your needs. Honesty and trust are a two-way street. We need to ensure we're also walking the talk when it comes to our values and acting as we want those to act toward us: clear communication, active listening, and respect.

Be Human.   Life happens, workplace issues happen. Managers have bad days. We have bad days. Besides all of this, remember we're all human; and drawing on the fundamentals of us sharing this human experience— where we all inherently have good intent and want the best for each other, workplace or otherwise—matters.

Behind the façade of the millennial person lies an untapped pool of skills and qualities—underpinned by a unique values system. A system that informs a new and different perspective of life and the world as they see it and what they want to come. Acknowledging and accepting that the contrast that exists is a pearl of opportunity to add value to any workplace and that it's possible to leverage all of this, only if managers are willing to listen. Key for managers and workplaces is to now act. Because with this newfound knowledge comes power—and with power, the possibility to make great things happen.

CHAPTER 2

The Millennial World

Top Challenges and Impacts to Workplaces

The Challenge

It's undeniable that we are living in increasingly challenging times. And while some would argue that it's a trend prevalent through history, the challenges that are being faced in the modern world today are different. For millennials, the challenges that are being faced and the respective pressure that it's placing on their lives are very real. We only need to look at the statistics—the rising rates of mental health challenges being an unnerving reminder of the complexity of what's going on underneath the surface of this generation. And while statistics are only one indicative measure, they're enough to say out loud: "Help me."

The challenges being faced are not isolated to an external bubble, meaning that workplaces will experience the offset—or unintended consequences—for the factors that impact millennials day to day. What this is presenting workplaces is an increasingly complex situation. How to manage (1) the external factors and challenges that affect the generation against (2) a different and more prominent set of values that demands different workplace spaces. Both through the operational day to day of how to operate remotely, and the human element which saw disruption to lives. Notwithstanding millennials had been gearing up—and advocating—for remote and flexible conditions—they were only slightly ahead of societal preparedness because of everything else that seemingly pulled them back in the opposite direction: financial challenges, mental health challenges, future of work challenges, and the unknown.

And it's the combined elements—challenges and values and now external/mental health issues—that present as pressing needs for workplaces. Asking—in fact, demanding—workplaces decide on "what" and "how" they will mitigate risk to performance, management, and operation for the people who are at the heart of the business: millennials.

The 2019 pandemic brought about a huge shift in ways of working, and perhaps in modern times, one of the biggest catalysts of workplace change. And while millennials had been advocating for more flexibility prior, the new set up to (almost) fully remote didn't occur without consequence. And those consequences, alongside the existing ones, are what workplaces are being challenged with—including what this means for them, and how to resolve them.

The Why

Living in our current society has demanded much change in the world. Change which will inevitably continue. From technological advancements to world politics to global economies, to health, to our planet—the world has seen drastic shifts and changes over the decades. For millennials, these external factors have played a key role in their lives—and like generations before, impact and influence in ways that are lasting.

The biggest shift for this generation is not so much the external factors but the way the values and approach to life (via conditioning and experience) has molded them. And one of the key areas is the absence of separation: the collective, wholistic, "all parts" perspective that they adopt and bring to their lives means that by default, the separation between external work and personal lives isn't like it used to be.

Fueled by a desire to operate with a more holistic approach to life, to support their own sense of finding fulfillment and meaning not just in work but their everyday lives. Their willingness to be more transparent, open, and expressive of their views complimenting this shift.

To truly appreciate the context and the state of being that millennials operate in means to understand the challenges by adopting a comparative stance for both history and their lives postpandemic.

Like most problems, to come up with a solution means to understand the why. It's this level of detail—the background, the context, the behind the scenes—that provides a "deep dive" into the heart of issues. In turn, allowing problems to be addressed in a meaningful way that don't just provide solutions to current challenges but create long-term sustainability for the future.

For some workplaces—if not many—investing in understanding their workforce hasn't been on the agenda. In fact, research supports that relative to other business priorities, it's been on the low list. And this is where the fundamental problem lies—the problem that supports the "why" and the criticality of the need to pivot and make understanding millennials a priority.

Investing in understanding your millennials is a must. Workplaces need to understand what factors, events, and situations have shaped this generation, including the gravity and depth of the challenges that impact their lives each day. It is not unless doing so, can workplaces understand how this translates to business; the impacts on those critical areas, like performance and productivity.

To find a solution means to understand the cause and effect. And it starts with a deep dive into millennial-specific challenges; looking at the world through the millennial lens.

Millennials have been trying to reconcile the challenges and complexities of everyday life for most of their existence. While 2022 is presenting unstable economic conditions, inflation, geopolitical conflicts, quality of life deterioration, and climate issues, these are not new. For millennials, these challenges have been longstanding; the exacerbation and levels of impact are the varying factors here.

To start with a blank canvas would be remiss, let alone lessen the contextual complexity with how these issues, including the present-day challenges, are being felt. Those areas can be divided into Finances, Education, Employment, and Mental Health.

The Past (Prepandemic)

Finances

The Global Financial Crisis (GFC) of 2008 was a huge culprit in affecting both the climate and financial challenges that millennials have experienced over the last decade or more. In fact, to understand the gravity, it was considered to have been the worst financial crisis since the Great Depression of the 1930s (pending the current situation postpandemic), with research supporting that millennials were hit the hardest by this. And while understanding the effects of the GFC on the millennial generation may not be complete, there are some truths which are evident. The summary being the economic crisis left permanent scars: a broken economy, no career progression, and consequences of a recession. In fact, many of the consequences remain active concerns.

Graduating into an economy of job scarcity, high unemployment, low wages, and a rising cost of living has been hugely challenging for millennials. Millennials graduated into a climate of reduced earning capability.[1] Reports indicate that the median incomes of households, especially those headed by millennials, fell up to 25 percent between 2007 and 2013, compared to the same age cohort in 2007.[2] The results saw millennials earn up to a quarter less than a decade ago (and trying to offset that against the rising cost of living and inflation). It wouldn't be so much of an issue if the cost of living hadn't also exceeded at the same time. Inflation increasing considerably in the past 20 years, exacerbated by the pandemic. Largely due to higher prices for oil, gasoline, transportation, and rent, it's also exacerbated by wage freezes and inflation rate rises. The housing crisis became a ticking time bomb for many economies—wiping out savings and increasing inequality, with low-cost housing continuing to disappear from the market. For decades, housing costs have risen faster than incomes; meaning this generation can be spending around 30 to 40 percent of wages on rent.

The solution for many millennials was—and has been—to accumulate more debt, and with the stress of affordability and financial situations, it has come at a cost to "life milestones" and "adulting." The recession caused many millennials to pause or defer major adult milestones—big life decisions and investments—such as buying a home, getting married,

---

[1] L.B. Kahn. 2010. "The Long-Term Labor Market Consequences of Graduating From College in a Bad Economy," *Labour Economics* 17, no. 2, pp. 303–316.

[2] Federal Reserve Bank. 2017. "Changes in U.S. Family Finances from 2013 to 2016: Evidence from the Survey of Consumer Finances," *Federal Reserve Bulletin* 103, no. 3, pp. 1–42.

and having kids. This saw a dramatic shift in the "timeline of events" (i.e., major milestones), which ordinarily would have happened—comparative to their parents—in their early twenties. Instead, these decisions have been deferred—for some well into their thirties.

Education

While millennials are the most educated generation in history—a statistic that should be valued—it has been offset by several factors. Despite progressive changes in the higher education sector—with the realization that skills and courses need to fit with both the current and future demands of work—many millennials haven't experienced this.

For those students of the 90s and 2000s, many felt the pressure to choose a course of study—often exacerbated by parents or societal expectations on what a career "should look like." The result saw many millennials embarking on careers, irrespective of whether they wanted it (and at the same time, accumulating significant amounts of student debt). And while the question has been asked for those affected—would that have chosen that career—the answer isn't the relevant part: It has been the pressure and "forced" pathway of tertiary education. Which didn't just affect the number of qualified candidates applying for jobs but gave employers the opportunity to hand pick the best of the best—exacerbating competition for jobs—all without a guaranteed end result.[3,4]

Employment

Statistically speaking, employment has been a challenge for millennials. Millennials who entered the job market during the worst of the crisis felt it. Not just the immediate effects but the way it influenced their career

---

[3] C.R. Hulten and V.A. Ramey. 2018. "Education, Skills, and Technical Change: Implications for Future US GDP Growth," University of Chicago Press. www.nber.org/books/hult-12.

[4] L.B. Kahn. 2010. *The Long-Term Labor Market Consequences of Graduating From College in a Bad Economy, Labour Economics* 17, no. 2, pp. 303–316. https://doi.org/10.1016/j.labeco.2009.09.002.

paths (as stated earlier). While up until the pandemic, marginal improvements had been made over the last decade, what has been obscured are the issues experienced: the market, wages, debt, and inequality.

The market millennials entered reflected a huge discrepancy between the number of jobs that were available versus the amount of job seekers. Employers were faced with hundreds of applicants for a single job opening. And while this competition would have probably been considered reflective of interest and a "healthy" market, it was driven mostly through desperation and need. Which meant that millennials weren't getting the jobs they wanted, even after graduation. They were—and in some parts are—still being forced into applying for jobs below their qualifications. Whether its college graduates applying for retail or coffee shop jobs, to lawyers and PhD graduates applying for entry-level research jobs, the job market forced many to lower sights and expectations. While temporary job agencies may have offered an alternative and seemingly "reliable" way to generate income between jobs, they stopped holding the weight they used to, purely due to competition.

The aging population—a sociological challenge that has been brewing over the last two decades—has also presented additional limitations. There is a growing share of older generations (e.g., Baby Boomers) who are not retiring. Not only due to improvement of life longevity and mortality rates but the current costs of living. And while trends will change over time, the current situation may mean millennials will need to think differently. Furthermore, the displacement of jobs has increased—with technology key to that. While the rise of automation has seen huge efficiencies for workplaces, there has been a human reduction factor in positions.

The global climate that exists now is still unreliable; however, what trends are indicating is the balance of power shifting: unemployment rates are high, not due to the job shortages but because of the "lack of interest," especially by younger generations who are "done" with old ways of working. Even before the pandemic inspired the Great Resignation (the current economic trend in which employees have voluntarily resigned from their jobs, to be covered in Chapter 2), millennials have always shown the highest rates of job dissatisfaction.[5] The issues have been manifold—and

---

[5] R. Ngotngamwong. 2020. *A Study of Millennial Job Satisfaction and Retention* 21, pp. 47–58.

while these will be covered more broadly in Chapter 5, at a high level, this dissatisfaction has stemmed from limitations in career progression, workload demands (burnout), and the perceived unwillingness of managers and workplaces to listen to wants and needs.

Mental Health

Millennials are at a higher risk of mental health challenges than any other generation. Unprecedented levels of anxiety and depression have made millennials quite literally a "generation on edge." Their sense of well-being across areas of health, relationships, and finances is low. Over time, they have been becoming more and more socially isolated, suffering significant drops in personal well-being. Even their sense of belonging has plummeted by over 30 percent in the last decade.[6] At least one in five will report depression in the workplace, and studies show that we are the most anxious generation—especially women.[7]

Reasons for this are varied and present a complex situation. First is due to the accumulation of the earlier challenges; second are personality traits that include perfectionism, overachievement due to reward attainment, and self-induced pressure; third, the offset of technology and social media influences like technology addictions and instant gratification syndrome; and finally, because the rates of reporting are more likely to have increased, given the pro-awareness and willingness to talk about mental health.

The Present (Postpandemic)

The current climate of the world and what this means for millennials can be summarized as uncertain, unstable, and complex. While millennials who experienced the effects of the 2008 GFC may feel a sense of dread at the familiarity of what is occurring around the globe on an economic level, the biggest effects will arguably be on the shoulders of Generation Z. Especially when it comes to the workplace. And while the

[6] D. Kingman. 2018. *New IF Research Shows That Young Adults' Wellbeing Has Fallen by 10% Since Mid1990s,* Intergenerational Foundation. www.if.org.uk/.
[7] Bensinger, DuPont, and Associates. 2015. *Anxiety and Work: The Impact of Anxiety on Different Generations of Employees.* https://us.morneaushepell.com/.

lasting impacts of the pandemic are yet to be determined, what is certain is that it has not alleviated any of the existing challenges. In some cases, it has simply exacerbated them.

Education

The pandemic prompted millennials into thinking about education from a different lens. Already wired for learning, the position that many found themselves in was available time. And whether in positions of redundancy or voluntary departures from their jobs, for a percentage of the generation, it was fundamentally a time of reassessment. The results saw businesses and side hustles launched or revived, new skills learned, and changes to job pathways. What also occurred was a re-examination of traditional routes to study; dissatisfaction from existing students regarding university and college responses not helping. Overall, prompting a re-examination of not just the institution of higher education but the education pathway itself—which now includes confidence in upskilling and educational development vis-à-vis self-learning, including via platforms that are easily accessible and familiar (e.g., YouTube).

Finances

Research indicates that the current struggle with the cost of living and financial concerns is the key concern for millennials.[8] Shockingly, almost half of millennials (47 percent) are living paycheck to paycheck, with up to a quarter (33 percent) having a second job (full or part time) to manage. The extension of concerns around savings and retirement are also prevalent, with more than a quarter (31 percent) not confident that they'll be able to retire comfortably. The wealth disparity, which was already creating inequality—an existing concern—is not reported to have increased, with more than three-quarters (77 percent) of millennials believing that the gap between the rich and the poor is growing.[9]

---

[8] Deloitte Insights. 2022. *The Deloitte Global 2022 Gen Z and Millennial Survey.*
[9] Ibid.

Employment

The Great Resignation—the event which has historically seen the most people quit their jobs in history—was arguably led by millennials.[10] Not least because of precedented dissatisfaction being faced but a newfound reassessment—and realignment—of their values and needs. The consequences of this mass exodus from the workforce have been felt around the world and are likely to continue for some time.

Mental Health

The rates of mental health challenges around the globe are at the highest in reported history. With millennials leading those statistics, the impacts of the pandemic have elevated these concerns for Generation Z—with studies suggesting that the baton will be passed along, as Generation Z's mental health challenges surpass millennials.

Mental health cannot be separated from the office. Lines have become blurred between personal and professional lives, and irrespective of whether people return to the office or stay remote, there isn't an off switch. This means there is a greater need from the workplace to support this. Looking to the causes outside of the factors discussed earlier, unsurprisingly, it's still the financial concerns that have millennials most concerned—with both long-term financial futures and day to day finances continuing to drive the top stress factors. The workload and overburdened pressures that millennials were facing in the workplace prior to the pandemic have been exacerbated, with burnout now being one of the top reasons for mental health challenges. In fact, almost half (45 percent) of millennials report feeling burned out due to the intensity of their working environments.

This burden of mental health challenges for these generations is undeniably at the forefront of global concerns. For workplaces, the impacts will be unavoidable. Rises in absenteeism, declines in performance and

---

[10] Workjam. 2022. *Millennials Far More Likely to Quit Jobs Than Gen Z, Bosses Say.* www.workjam.com/newsroom/bloomberg-millennials-far-more-likely-to-quit-jobs-than-gen-z/.

productivity, financial costs of benefits, and reductions in general morale and culture are all on the upward trend.

Management Best Practices

What Millennials Want

For a generation experiencing significant challenges, there is simplicity in what they want from managers. Outside of their workplace expectations and wants, millennials **want managers to listen, acknowledge their challenges, hear their concerns, and offer support.** This also extends to acknowledgment of what they are trying to do to minimize some of the issues. At the core, millennials are a generation who are flexible, adaptable, and solution-oriented. The current challenges demand that they think outside the box. Not just on an individual level but collectively as a generation. And as times would dictate, they have been able to adapt, pivot, and, in some ways, offer some innovative ways of doing things different.

From a financial perspective, millennials have had to change their spending habits. This has meant deferring purchasing choices on things like houses or cars, which traditionally support the economy. These delayed purchases have been born out of a necessity, with existing debt and cost of living taking priority and the inability to save for deposits.

The ripple effect of this has also seen this generation stay in the family home much longer, as they try to save or minimize the costs of living. In fact, following the 2008 GFC, some millennials took refuge in moving back under the roof of their parents—a trend which was adopted again during the recent pandemic, which saw a huge millennial and Gen Z migration back to their family homes.

Realizing that money alone may not always get them what they want, or need, millennials have sought other ways to get returns on investment, or equivalent rewards or value. This includes their existing purchases, which have placed greater emphasis on brand loyalty and rewards. This also extends to the value of a product or service—a consideration which has become a key component in their purchasing decision making. Aware of their financial limitations, they are choosing wisely, with a reluctance to spend on a product or service without a clear expectation of value.

More globally, they have revolutionized the sharing economy, or what is known as collaborative consumption where people share, ride, and borrow collectively. Services like co-working spaces, car-sharing services, and house-sharing are supported not only due to financial incentives that reduce costs but also because of their conscious consumerism mindset, which places weight on the environment and sustainability.

Getting to the crux of what millennials want: The tagline is, a financial break. And while experiential living aside—including jokes about "higher end" purchases, such as avocado consumption, gluten-free choices, and organic coffee—the reality is this generation is aware of the money-pinching feelings to live a "normal life." There is frustration felt; the third recession being experienced for some millennials, which means constant rebudgeting and re-evaluation of lifestyle choices is occurring, adding to stress. Millennials don't want to be living in the confides or the constraint of dollars but recognize it is part of life. **What they want from their workplaces, and managers, is acknowledgment that for some, times are indeed tough, that money does matter, and where possible and able, to offer support.**

From an employment perspective, the Great Resignation aside, there are several approaches millennials are taking to their employment situation. Assessing the loyalty of their employers—which might be under the guise of asking for a raise, taking a secondment, or enrolling in a course to upskill. Not to be confused with entitlement, this loyalty testing vis-à-vis requests is also a way of helping millennials come to determine their own value and worth if they haven't worked that out yet. The process itself can also provide a valuable learning opportunity and character-building generally.

In workplaces **where dissatisfaction is being felt, millennials are most likely to leave than stay.** For those that remain however, and especially in situations where agreements have been made and are yet to come to fruition (absent, delayed, or otherwise), they will hold managers to account. That "hold to account" is likely to take the form of "requires explanation," a new demand and/or chance to renegotiate to re-establish trust.

For those in existing roles, there will likely be further demands placed on managers and workplaces. This will be particularly evident in workplaces where there is no viable career pathway. These demands may be a press on boundaries, especially when it comes to time spent working at home, flexible hours, or even monetary values. Better culture and ways of working have also become paramount, which includes support from managers.

From an education perspective, millennials have an innate need to learn—and it is something that they place great value in. Formal education or otherwise, they understand the financial commitment that comes with study. For those already experiencing the weight of student debt, even more so.

Millennials are also acutely aware of the time commitment needed to invest in study pathways, and, in turn, the outcome of what they'll eventually achieve. This is why they place emphasis on quality in getting what they pay for and in some cases push for more. Traditional routes aside, millennials are also more willing to look at alternative ways of educating and upskilling. Online courses, weekend workshops, mentoring, apprenticeships—it isn't necessarily the route taken that matter to millennials but the quality of what they get, both through the experience and the outcome. What this means for workplaces is that **millennials want to ensure that career progression is on the agenda and part of their performance development; that they have goals to work toward.** Particularly important for those millennials who might not have the means or ability to invest, they'll look at how they can leverage their workplace by using existing resources—such as internal training and development—to support their development.

From a mental health perspective, managers must understand that external stressors aside, there are millennial-specific characteristics which add complexity to the challenges around mental health. And while these characteristics largely manifest through behaviors, there is no denying the severity of the internalization.

Pressure

Millennials place themselves under enormous amounts of pressure. Not helped by their upbringing, there are other causations that have weaved themselves into the mix. The "yes" factor, which is often a seemingly innocent result of the want to try or experience something new, or seeing the potential value it may add to their lives, to Fear of Missing Out (FOMO), is not helped by social media, with the consequence leading to overwhelm. Managers need to be aware of this—including where it's most likely going to show up. Overcommitting to work, not speaking up when the workload is too much, operating in a silo, and not asking for help.

Perfectionism

Millennials have a stronger perfectionist trait than other generations.[11] This overburden is also exacerbated by the multifaceted aspect: pursuits of flawlessness, setting high standards and expectations, and the critical tendency to review themselves. For these reasons, it will manifest through laboring over tasks, indecision, internalization, worrying about what people think, and questioning worth or esteem.

Dissatisfaction

Millennials have spent their lives striving for goals and rewards. This conditioned behavior-response has had adverse effects on their feelings of satisfaction, mostly via reward depletion. Which means reaching the threshold for gratification is continuing to move further ahead. The constant strives and pressure to achieve more by taking on extra work or tasks, education, or setting unrealistic goals are what we see in the workplace.

That said, **millennials are increasingly taking control of their mental health**. Well-being has become paramount to their existence and is now a part of their day to day. Not only have this generation been advocates for changing the status quo and stigma around mental health awareness, but they are increasingly taking on responsibility for themselves—and their generation. This includes being aware of factors that impede mental health and well-being, like the use of technology, social media consumption, workload pressure, and their own expectations. From digital detoxes to advocating for mental health initiatives, taking

---

[11] T. Curran and A.P. Hill. 2017. "Perfectionism Is Increasing Over Time: A Meta-Analysis of Birth Cohort Differences From 1989 to 2016," *Psychological Bulletin*.

"mental health days," canceling social plans, to the extremes of quitting jobs for organizations that don't make mental health an active priority.

How to Support

Against understanding the causal factor that makes millennials them, how this translates into the workplace is through an undeniable question: What does this mean for me, and how can I, as a manager, provide support?

From a Financial Perspective

Often outside of the control of workplaces, there are ways to support and ease the burden for millennials.

Assess Needs

If able, gauge the financial needs of your millennials. For example, if you know they live far from the office or need to put their children in child care, support them by developing ways of working that mitigate some of the strain. It could be as simple as letting millennials work from home more often to save the cost of travel or child care.

Flexible Schedule

Understand that millennials may be working a second job to support themselves or their family. Managers can help support workloads and stress by setting more practical and realistic deadlines or providing more flexibility in working hours.

Financial Incentives

Already reward-driven, millennials welcome the opportunity to earn more money. Managers can help support by marrying up performance with bonuses and financial incentives that encourage them both personally and professionally.

From an Employment Perspective

Careers and work matter to millennials. Outside of the challenges being faced by this generation, they strive for a workplace that gives them the ability to show up and add value.

Understand Values

Get to know what is important to your millennials—their values, needs, and motivators—and then work with them to develop an environment that allows them to thrive.

Support Their Ambitions

The need to be heard in the workplace, extends to support for their ambitions and goals. The easiest way to do this is to help them articulate their goals and then build them into a performance plan.

Identify Value

Millennials want to be able to see and feel where they can add value—both in their job and their interactions with colleagues. Helping them identify where they can make a unique contribution, or expressing more recognition of their existing contribution, will support their desire and continued drive.

From an Education Perspective

Millennials are a generation who thrive on learning, development, and opportunities. However, statistics indicate that workplaces are not investing anywhere near enough into this.[12] And while the impacts from a retention and recruitment perspective will be discussed later, this need for growth is critical to nurture and should be offered.

---

[12] "Are We Trained For Work? Employee and Practitioner Perspectives on UK L&D." 2022. www.digits.co.uk/are-we-trained-for-work-confirmation/ (accessed October 2022).

Identify Wants

This ties in with career progression and should be part of the performance plan. For workplaces, more broadly, these learning and development opportunities should fall in part of a People Plan or Human Resource Plan that sets objectives into supporting the future growth and skills of the organization. Identifying needs and skills gaps, in addition to listening to what your millennials want, will enable you to develop a plan that doesn't just support the appetite of millennials but future performance and growth.

Nurture Talent

Recent years have seen more focus by workplaces and educational providers to ensure they are identifying the future skills and needs of the workforce. This has also extended to thinking of new ways to recruit talent. In doing so, workplaces have begun to form partnerships with higher education institutes or develop their own accredited qualification and courses. This "grass roots" approach not only offers workplaces a unique way of developing their own workforce but also a meaningful way of giving existing employees the opportunity to develop.

From a Mental Health Perspective

The key to managing the current dynamic is setting up strategies to support millennials. Doing so means that millennials can support themselves, engage in a more meaningful way, and, most importantly, free up some of the managerial challenges being faced.

Shift Attitude

The world has moved into an era where talking about issues that matter are discussed. Mental health is one of those. While the past may have seen older generations "get on with it," this mentality doesn't stand up today. Not when there are services and systems to help.

Prioritize Mental Health

Managers have a responsibility to create a work environment that supports mental health needs. Which means it should be built into workplace strategy, policies, or processes.

Encourage an Inclusive Culture

Fostering open and inclusive workplaces where people feel comfortable and supported talking about mental health is critical. Managers can start small (such as putting it onto a workplace meeting agenda) if needed.

Emotional Support

Acting in ways that can alleviate feelings of pressure, perfectionism, and dissatisfaction is important. Open dialogue, assessment of workloads, and helping set boundaries; encouraging decision making, fostering "shades of grey" thinking, and offering a safe space for opinions; balancing "to do" lists with realistic expectations, avoiding allocating too much work, and encouraging nonemotive rationale thinking.

Set Up Support Systems

Whether these are in-house or through external service providers, having support systems available is critical. This includes making sure employees know who is available to contact and when.

For Millennials: How to Get What You Want

Global challenges aside, part of the solution to this lies with us. Educated, aware, or otherwise, there are things that we can do to mitigate the external and support our workplaces and managers to better enable us to get what we need and want.

Sure, we've got parents who were (or still are) too involved in our lives. There may have been times when we've been falsely led to believe that everyone will acknowledge our efforts, no matter how big or small. And yes, not all of us have felt adequately prepared for the "real world" when we've stepped out on our own and faced the existential challenges around us—including our jobs. But regardless of our position right now, whether we've pushed the boundaries of our own desires, or not, it's probably fair to say that there might be a part that feels victimized by it all.

However, this doesn't make us any less individual or hinders the choices and power we have to create and live the life we want. We must recognize and accept that we, as a generation, have been raised in a world that is, and will continue to be, vastly different from decades gone by. Our generation is facing a different set of challenges than other generations because of a different set of conditions. And whether we like it or not, our world as we know it is defined by uncertainty and unpredictably.

We must shift our perspective and find an alternative viewpoint to the world as we know it. And in doing so, take responsibility, let go, and move forward. Irrespective of who we've become or what has happened to bring us to this point, our generation is united by these experiences. Experiences which do not define who we are but help provide context to our lives and, in some cases, answers to questions.

Our life experience and the events happening around have affected us in ways we haven't realized. But gifted with the power of knowledge, we can do something about it. Co-creating a better workplace and world. **To navigate these challenges and to create and build meaningful lives starts with perspective**. It isn't a time to play victim of circumstances; instead, it's a time to conquer. By our pure becoming, we have broken a mold of tradition, challenged the status quo, and redefined what normal would or could look like. And it's these very characteristics and traits that we have that allow us to manage the climate with ease.

From a Financial Perspective

We all know that "for things to change, we have to change." To deal with uncertain times and continue to manage our situation, it's important we recognize that personal responsibility, discipline, financial education, and desire to succeed are important. How to get ahead at work? **Talk about your needs with your manager.** Use what's in front of you and look at what benefits exist. Super, paid leave, conditions, health care. Ask for that raise, or be open to finding new ways to reduce expenses. Play an active part in creating the conditions that support your financial state.

From an Employment Perspective

If the pandemic didn't present everyone with an opportunity to take stock of our workplaces and careers, then nothing ever will. With our generation at the front edge of the Great Resignation and paving the way forward for a better working life, signals the fact that we've reached that point of realization where the things that don't work must stop. It's important that during this adjustment—because this transition phase will take time—we're not treating our workplaces as the enemy. **We, along with our workplaces, have an equal responsibility to work together to create an environment that nurtures us, with the exchange that our workplaces get the best out of us.**

We have the power to influence, respectively, and call for positive change in a way that brings harmony. Which means that for those of our generation who are choosing to remain in jobs where challenges exist, then the responsibility is on you for the call to action. Irrespective of the current climate, there is opportunity everywhere, and we can have the working lives and meaningful careers that we desire if we choose that.

From an Education Perspective

We know that education matters: the pursuit of learning and development. Our education doesn't have to take the "formal" route. In fact, if we adopt a resourceful approach and look at our existing environments, we may find there are opportunities already around—like the workplace which offers internal training, courses, higher duties, or acting positions. It might be deciding to upskill by creating a project or a "side hustle"— or for those existing to refine, or refresh us, with a "how can we do this better" mentality. We know it's not always about the money with these projects or ventures, as much as it is the satisfaction we have from creating and learning new skills. **Understanding where our interests lie and getting clear on what we want to achieve is key** to being able to use our educational pathways to support our life and careers.

From a Mental Health Perspective

Stress and pressure happen—it's life. However, the reality we can't avoid, or hide from, is that the world today is presenting a plethora of challenges for us that are impacting our mental health; to levels and degrees that haven't been seen before. We need to start thinking about the "why" and being more conscious of how we are living our lives: our emotions, our reactions, and what we're consuming from the external world. It's up to all of us to take responsibility for our well-being and, where needed, adjust our lives. Mental health challenges are not insurmountable and can be mitigated through awareness, education, and a concerted effort to put ourselves first.

As a generation, we have grown up with increased attention on mental health challenges. We talk about it, know people impacted by it, hear about it in the news, and see it play out in books, TV shows, and movies. While not quite "pop culture" in the traditional sense, the topic is contemporary—which means that the support out there is plenty. The slackening of stigma around mental health is something we can take advantage of. We shouldn't be in a position today where we're vilifying our aversive emotions and fighting them. We don't need to try to bury feelings like anxiety and stress. While admittedly, we are a generation who are hard on ourselves, we are in a prime position to be able to use these benefits of an inclusive society of people, where support is there if we need it.

Taking ownership over our mental health is a choice—and when it comes to the workplace, we must prioritize it. With the right knowledge and tools, we can make proactive decisions to honor our well-being both in the workplace and our lives.

Check in With Yourself

Asking yourself intentional questions such as how you feel in yourself (physically and emotionally) is a good start. In workplaces, it is easy to get caught up in being busy, which means we lose connection with ourselves. Taking a couple of short breaks per day to check in with yourself will help prevent feelings of overwhelm and give you the opportunity to deal with minor issues at the time.

Understand Your Limits and Set Realistic Goals

When you know what your limits are, it is easier to set a realistic and achievable workload. Being aware of the millennial predisposition to pressure and perfectionism will ensure that you are making mindful decisions that align with a healthy workload.

Speak Up

Too often we find ourselves in stressful situations that could have been avoided simply by communicating our needs. If you are feeling the pinch, tell your manager. Learn how to say "no." Reach out to mental health services that offer a space to simply unload. Communicating your wants and needs is critical.

Our world is a complex place, but with that complexity comes value: an opportunity for growth. If we are to take a moment and reflect on what the world has offered—and continues to offer—it is evident that workplaces have a huge opportunity to create a sustainable future for the millennial workforce. Leaders have a unique opportunity to embrace challenges, pivot, and invent new ways to manage—adding a new flair. Millennial teams have the opportunity to use their workplaces as a stable foundation for finding solution—or at the very least, a space where they feel supported to show up, challenges in toe.

Until workplaces and managers can appreciate the past challenges and presenting environment that millennials are in, they cannot provide solutions—or leverage the best out of them. **Exciting times exist—and the key for managers and their teams is to use the world not as an excuse but as a way to work closer, and more harmoniously, to build stronger foundations for success.**

CHAPTER 3

Millennials in the Workplace

Career and Expectations

The Challenge

The world of work is rapidly changing—and so too are careers. The future skills need to tackle global challenges, including the changing needs of the world, in the process of being redefined. And this process will continue to become the norm, as we move toward a more integrated, collaborative way of working with employers, government, sector, and higher education institutions. To prepare for the changes means manager needs to be ready to have these conversations with their millennial (and Generation Z) teams, to address what their careers look like now, and what they expect will come in the future.

The millennial view of the workplace, their careers, and expectations are the top issues that workplaces find challenging. On face value it doesn't appear overly complex. A career is a career, and progression happens when it happens, right? Not entirely. While workplaces can appreciate that millennials present with differing views and values, they are not necessarily au fait with how this translates into what they want from a career; the connection to expectations and desires; the impacts on retention and recruitment of talent; and the conflict and tension that may arise via intergenerational differences. The results being seen in the current challenges across workplaces: managing expectations, managing intergenerational diversity, and retention and recruitment. Challenges which interweave together.

When we consider that millennials will make up to 75 percent of the global workforce in the next five years, the criticality of understanding this generation becomes clear. They will be driving and shaping the growth of organizations and will be in control of creating impact and change. Intentional or not, the reality is that some workplaces are unable or unwilling to take the time to invest in their workforce by listening to the needs of their younger generations and understanding the core values system which drives them.

For many workplaces, trying to manage the career expectations of millennials is becoming increasingly difficult. Not just the management of their seeming "impatience" and want for rapid career progression, but how to manage their performance and engagement around these issues— especially when expectations haven't yet been discussed or set. Part of the problem is the inability to invest time in understanding career objectives, and the "why" behind these. Ignorance perhaps, influencing assumptions that all employees, regardless of age or experience, want the same thing out of their job. And that employees will adopt the same way of working and fit (or comply) with the status quo regardless of whether it truly fits their values, wants, or need.

In addition to expectations is the challenge presented by intergenerational diversity—specifically the complexity that comes with understanding a multiaged workforce. The consequence of "inability to" often seen via intergenerational conflict and tensions that arise between co-workers. One of the biggest is between Boomers and millennials: Those who may have "served time the hard way" versus the "need it now" mentality of wanting to see results and rewards in real time. In fact, studies suggest that almost 70 percent of employers believe that this level of ambition and desire is the leading cause of conflict between generations.[1]

Finally, there are retention and recruitment challenges (to be discussed in Chapter 6). As much as the pandemic challenged the hypothesis that most employees are committed to their jobs, the already known situation for millennials is that they are least committed than any generation to stay in one place of employment place for long. Workplace dissatisfaction aside, there is an inherent desire for this generation to learn and develop, both personally and professionally. Which means workplaces may need

---

[1] Robert Walters Whitepaper. 2022. *Attracting and Retaining Millennial Professionals*. www.robertwalters.com.

to reset expectations and get used to the fact that the average turnover rate for millennials is approximately two years. Meaning workplaces need to think differently about retention and recruitment of this generation. The simple questions being: "How can our workplace attract and retain quality talent?" leading to "What can our workplace offer to millennials that nurture their needs, while keeping them engaged as long as possible?" The ability to attract, retain, and leverage millennial talent is tied with the "what's in it for me" and "can I get what I need to nurture my career" thinking that millennials are already considering before they enter the workplace.

Despite the projected statistics and millennials rising into middle or senior management positions, the reality is if approaches to working with millennials or investment into understanding this generation aren't achieved, then challenges will continue to exist. Most, if not all, that translates into risk around productivity, performance, and people. Getting clear on what having a career means for millennials, what they expect from their workplace, and in turn want is critical.

The Why

For many workplaces, understanding why millennials have an exacerbating need to excel, expand, and get what they want is perplexing. It's not just managers who struggle to understand, but other (older) colleagues because the approach that millennials take to their careers could be arguably seen to be ruthless. They know what they want, and they are persistent to get it. And with that persistence comes the ask—and it's *this* that workplaces and managers often find disconcerting. Not just the "request" (which may feel like a demand) but their ability to challenge "why" or "why not"—unintentionally projecting what mistakenly is perceived as entitled, impatient, and disrespectful attitudes. The push for an explanation, the want to implement new strategies, the need for timelines and commitments, and the negotiations that go with all of these are leaving managers surprised and perplexed. Both at the "audacious challenges" but the additional pressures on their own accountability and transparency.

However, if we break down the approach and this seemingly challenging behavior in the workplace, we can build a basis for understanding, and with that, a new perspective. One that demonstrates that **what millennials want from their career and workplace is intrinsically tied to their values and needs**. How this translates, means they want jobs and workplaces that support their values and allow them to live them each day. Which is why understanding the core drivers of these values and how this translates into behaviors, attitudes, and skills is critical.

The role of values is intrinsic, and for millennials, these act as core motivators: a north star which governs choices, actions, and decisions. What drives them, what excites them, what gets them up in the morning is the very energy that needs to be canvassed, not just about the workplace or within the varying degrees of separation in the office, but to the wider world. They have the power to fuel rockets, and the minds and ideas to make anything happen. And their willingness to sidestep the traditional ways of operating, their incessant ability to continue to overcome hurdles, and use opportunities to make it work for them, is part of why they are a power generation.

Managing Retention and Recruitment

So how do the values of millennials shape their approach to the workplace and career they strive for? Millennials are an individualistic generation, which means they value their own personal growth and skill development as a priority for their careers. While job security and stability are important, it's not a key consideration that millennials are thinking about when making choices about companies to join or, in fact, what types of jobs or careers they want. This is a different approach from older generations.

Further, millennials aren't tied to the idea of obtaining a fixed, specific role or moving up the ranks of what are the traditional hierarchical structures. Instead, they are focused on finding a job that aligns with who they are. Their interest in the corner office with the skyline city views and "CEO" plaque on the door is less than their interest in the opportunity to take a "perceived sideways" step or a new task or project that will add value to their career and experience. Which is why they are less likely to stay with one employer throughout their lives.[2] They know when a job

---

[2] Price Waterhouse Coopers (PWC). 2022. *Workforce of the Futures. The Competing Forces Shaping 2030.* https://pwc.to/2Rfozuq.

isn't serving its purpose anymore. And while there is something to be said about the responsibility of workplaces retaining millennials, there is also simply the desire they have, to expand knowledge.

Millennials are programmed for giving and getting value. The world and the existing environment that millennials are part of cannot be excluded from the equation. Outside of the core need to make the world a better place—an innate value—they are consciously aware of the current state of the world: political, economic, social, and environment. It is perhaps, the people and planet aspects that gain the attention of millennials most when it comes to their working lives. And that being the appeal of working with organizations or having jobs that make a direct impact on society in a positive way, such as social enterprises and sustainable business.[3]

It's for this reason that workplaces would benefit strongly from ensuring that core values around brand and impact and not just articulated but embodied. And while all of this might seem like a selfish approach to work and career, millennials don't see it that way. Instead, they simply value their lives and the standards and goals they have.

Managing Expectations: The Why

Many of us have heard the saying that "we become the product of our parents." And for many millennials, this rings true; an unfortunate offset of the environment they were raised in.

Helicopter parenting—a term which gained the most attention when millennials were entering college (i.e., the early 2000s)—and was never intended to do harm. However, the adverse effects of overparenting were never articulated—at least not in a way that was readily understood, especially in the long term. What began as seemingly harmless attention (albeit excessive) of their child's experience in the formative years turned into intrusive behavior as they reached teenage years and early adulthood. The wanting better for their children to have the best, their attempts to engineer a picturesque life, vis-à-vis interfering and involvement, had the

---

[3] C. Phillips and J. Hopelain. 2015. *What Do Millennials Want in a Job? Insights for Making Talent Brands Millennial-Relevant* (Brand Amplitude, LLC).

unduly consequence of stripping away their independence. And in turn, the critical skills that workplaces need: like critical thinking, creativity, and resilience.

For millennials, this absence of tools to help support them in the workplace, coupled with the perception and **illusion of what their jobs, careers, and life in the workplace would entail versus the actuality, has been a huge reality check**. With the umbilical cord of support from parents cut, and facing new situations, has resulted in many millennials (and their parents) having to complete an overhaul of expectations and reality.

Managing Intergenerational Tension

The "need for now" versus "paying dues" is a bugbear for many workplaces. To understand this, we must look at the circumstances around this.

Technology

Millennials have grown up in an era teeming with tech. They are the first generation to have been raised with computers and smartphones and witnessed the evolution of social media. They have become everyday experts in seeking out answers to just about every question via the Internet. And as a result, technology has become completely unified into their everyday lives. **From a workplace perspective, what this means is millennials expect technology to do their jobs.**

Admittedly, this expectant need has appeared under the guise of entitlement; however, it's not the case. All millennials want are the tools they need to do their job effectively and efficiently. Not helped by the pace of life, the introduction and continuation of the expansion of technology mean that this generation is not just conditioned for accessibility to information but the pleasure principle of an "on demand" world. And while becoming a global phenomenon, it is undeniable that the roots of this are embedded in the use of technology.

Instant Gratification Syndrome

Exacerbating technology is instant gratification syndrome; as it sounds, a condition, an illness, or even an addiction for many. There are examples everywhere: food, entertainment, online shopping, and even dating have been engineered to make it easy for people to obtain whatever they want, whenever they want. For millennials, this technology and social media duo, alongside their own expectations of what they want from their careers, means that the likelihood of them being able to demonstrate patience becomes a challenge. **One thing that most millennials share is whatever they want, they want quickly.** They've been accustomed to a world where everything happens on demand. And when they don't get what they want or can't find fulfillment, they become anxious, tense, and irritable people.

Why millennials are the way they are when it comes to career and expectations is because of conditioning, values, and environment. That aside, **the solutions lie in millennials and managers recognizing each other.** Having more appreciation for the intrinsic and external factors influencing this generation encourages a willingness to create positive workplace cultures and change.

Management Best Practices

What Millennials Want

First and foremost, millennials want to be taken seriously, treated like adults, and be heard. This includes what they want and expect from their work and careers. Millennials are a generation who enter the workplace with drive and ambition. They have a desire for ownership over their careers (and lives). The key for managers is to recognize and understand that outside of their conditioned upbringing, the skills that they may or may not have, or whatever other preconceived notions or experience that exist, they want to be treated with maturity and respect for the individual they are. Irrespective of their age or "demonstrated" experience.

Millennials are focused on ensuring that their careers and the workplaces they choose to be part of are matching their expectations and providing them with opportunity to continue to grow and develop. As a result, many will push for a partnership way of working to ensure that their needs, alongside the needs of their workplace, are being met. And while it's not the traditional approach that workplaces may be used to, it's an approach that they must adjust to—not least to keep their millennials engaged and performing but retained.

Millennials expect largely that their managers and workplaces will hear what they have to say, and where needed adapt or change to ways where they have identified are not of great value (e.g., ways of working or process). Not intended as disrespectful, but a want to be more effective, efficient, and productive in how they go about their day. Their personal lives have already offered them a platform for efficiencies—reflected in how they use technology to support their lifestyles in a seamless way of working. Thus, as part of this integration into the workplace, they find that showing up in workplaces where systems, process, or technology are largely outdated, or there is an unwillingness for workplaces to adopt an open mind to new ways of working, thinking, or doing, then they'll not just look for new opportunities elsewhere, but while doing so, disengage.

Millennials want to be able to bring their whole selves to work—which means integrating parts of their career with their lives. They expect to have the flexibility to grow in and out of roles—as they do with living adaptable and flexible lives in general. They expect that their managers will provide them with a level of security and "comfort,"—a platform that ensures they feel supported to take steps toward their goals.

Key for managers is getting to know the whole entity—the person—of who that millennial is. Which is broader than who they are in their assigned role or job in the workplace. It extends to where their interests and other skills lie. This generation has a huge degree of flexibility and adaptability, and with their quick uptake of learning new skills, often supported by technology and online platforms, they're a generation who bring more to a workplace then what's on face value.

Getting the best out of millennials means taking a holistic view and recognizing all they bring to the workplace. And it's this recognition—the acknowledgment that millennials live multifaceted lives with work being only one element—is something they want. And this is where leveraging the best out of the person is realized: because when millennials feel like they are understood, they will give everything they have and then some.

How to Support

The how to help empower millennials on their career pathway, which in turn supports your role as a manager and the overall workplace, means adopting various approaches. None of which are exclusive but to be seen as complimentary to each other.

Listen to Their Needs

We know millennial needs may be complex, which is why dedicating specific time to asking the right questions is important. For example, one of the areas millennials find challenging is the transition from higher education (i.e., universities and colleges) to the workplace, especially when they are graduating into entry-level roles, which they find challenging. While agreed there is a starting point for a career, there are nuisances in this; not least because this generation isn't cut from a mold of "doing things as they once were" but because of the multifaceted issues at play—and the clash. Influenced by parental and societal expectations, technology, social media, and their own self-regulation.

In some cases, **millennials may need help articulating what they want from their career.**

One of the challenges that workplaces find themselves in—not least because of this reason—is a pool of millennials who are flittering about, changing minds or direction, and not being certain in any one way. To counter this and provide the support they need, communication is vital. And as managers, this extends beyond the ability to listen and provide insight and guidance. It's demonstrating what you know and understand about where their values, skills, and passions lie. In turn, supporting in identifying their needs, including where their strengths and weakness lie, is helpful. Furthermore, this approach makes them feel appreciated, vis-à-vis the time invested by their manager in listening.

Set Expectations in a Meaningful Way

In cases where expectations between millennials and managers don't match up, or problems are apparent, **what they appreciate and respect most is transparency, honesty, and understanding "why."** As managers, articulate "why" or "why not" something isn't possible. And while it's not to say they'll be happy with an outcome of "no," what they value is understanding the why. However, rather than let them hang, provide an alternative solution, or work with them to create one. They will be far more willing to work with managers in anticipation that whatever problem they are facing or limitation with getting their career to a satisfying point, there is an end goal—even if some compromise needs to occur.

Let Them Figure It Out

Millennials are programmed for natural problem solving—but they need the environment that supports this. Oftentimes this doesn't happen. While a permission to fail approach will be discussed later, one thing that managers can do to support millennial career exploration is to let them figure out what they want. This might sound like a counterintuitive approach, but to undo the parental conditioning and beliefs means managers may have to step out of the way. And while they will experience disappointment, this act of "tough love" will help them understand what it's like to overcome and learn from failure. This also includes, where able, **allowing them to make decisions and experience the consequences, both positive and negative, of their choices.**

Build on Their Desire for Intrinsic Motivation

Millennials have been dubbed the "trophy" generation and for good reason. The external motivation to achieve, which stems back to their school experience, saw rewards and recognition provided just for the sheer effort of showing up: the participation ribbon. Some of the consequence of this has been the association between reward and the least amount of effort. Which means to counter and drive performance, managers must look to intrinsic motivators instead, **understanding their vision, purpose,** and how as managers, you can help support their career desires.

Provide Support

The reality that many workplaces are facing is the high risk of turnover of millennials through the lack of support given to support their career objectives. And while the phrase, "Get on the train or get out of the way," may conjure up the very pinnacle of millennial entitlement, it's not designed to be that way but rather a simple, albeit blunt statement that might be helpful. Managers must understand that millennials are on a pathway to progress, which means that things that get in their way, they will find a way around. Being on the train doesn't mean you have to agree with their views or approach, but it allows you to work with them vis-à-vis support—**an enabler to help them develop**—rather than the blocker who gets in their way, inevitably risking retention.

Equally fitting is the phrase, "Pick your battles." For managers, being informed of which battle (if any) to pick is helped vastly by understanding the fundamental wants and needs that millennials have regarding their careers. In addition, there's added benefit for managers who do find themselves in positions of challenge or struggle in that it provides an opportunity to learn the art of letting go. Which means rather than resist the struggle with millennials, having awareness and understanding of who they are, allows one to simply let go.

Think Future Skills and Careers

Respecting that the current career pathway millennials have, or aspire to create, may not be the one they end up with. This isn't residual impact of the 2008 GFC with some millennials being moved into careers they may not have otherwise chosen, but the fact that **the future workplace, and the skills that are needed, may be different from the now**. The benefit for workplaces—especially those who can think ahead and plan strategically—is the ability to work with current teams on upskilling and fast tracking through to new pathways that are relevant. Something that millennials will both warm to and want, given they'll have already been thinking, planning, or are currently studying or upskilling in areas that aren't just of interest to them but align with the future world.

For some workplaces, a strategic approach that could be considered may be going direct to the source: that being the higher education provider. Recent advancements across industry and sector are seeing a new commitment for government, industry, and employers to work together. And in doing so, developing a graduate recruitment program that not just helps the future careers of millennials (and Generation Z) but also allows workplaces to select and build their own talent.

For Millennials: How to Get What You Want

As a generation who are built for progression, careers included, it's important we leverage what we're good at: adaptable, flexible, and strategic. Wherever you're placed on the spectrum of age, education, life, and professional experience, we all have one thing in common: the pursuit for learning, development and expansion doesn't die a quiet death just because we get older. In fact, for some of us, we become even more ready and willing to refine or redefine what our careers look and feel like for us. The pandemic, of course, helped those of us stuck, by giving us time to reexamine our lives and then act in meaningful ways.

Get Clear on What You Want

For us to truly get what we want out of our careers means to **understand what we want and why we want it**. Only then can we work out the "how" to go about it—allowing us to more readily, and easily, work toward creating our career pathway. This also means when it comes to our current (or future) workplaces, we need to be part of the solution. So rather than throw up expectations of what we want, work with our managers and workplaces to achieve those things. And while we may on the inside feel smug about the fact that we do hold a lot of power and leverage, we must use that leveraging stick in a fair and equitable way that is to the advantage of all.

We know that life changes quickly, so do we. However, for some of us, the instant gratification that we seek—in addition to constant ideas, the platforms to experiment, and "new shiny things" all around us—can make it very difficult to remain fixed on any one point. Which is why we need to demonstrate a little girt—both in the determining of what we want for the foreseeable future and our readiness and commitment to stick at it. If we aren't clear on what we want, or are too indecisive or uncommitted, then we can't speak up and have the conversation we need to with our managers to get what we want.

Plan (With Flexibility)

Not to diminish the "c'est la vie" and "live and let live" approach to our lives, there is a need for us to plan. This isn't just because it's a helpful approach to getting things done, but because we—the goal setting and extrinsic motivated sides of us—need something to work toward. The best way to do this is set up a plan with goals—short, medium, and as "long term" as we're realistically able to factor in. Key to our plans is also the need to adopt a flexible mindset and where needed (or wanted) to adjust. There's nothing wrong with pivoting from the plan or factoring in a couple of new milestones—like new opportunity. Remember that **our careers are a collective of what we experience and want, not a linear pathway.**

Communicate Your Needs

While having a conversation with our managers may feel daunting, the fact is, if we don't articulate what we want, then we're at risk of limiting the success of that happening. Career discussions shouldn't be something to shy away from; in fact, they should be inspiring and something we want to be talking about. **Having open and honest dialogue with our managers is key to this.** But equally so, understanding our own position and how we've been conditioned—which means having to manage our own expectations. Not all workplaces or managers are going to "get us," so we need to exercise patience, commitment, and persistence in getting to those things we set out to achieve. There is no same or next day service on our careers, rather a gradual accumulation and progression that we should value and take pride in—especially given the efforts.

Take Ownership

Key to moving ahead with our goals, careers, and pursuits is the simple fact that to get where we want to go, **we need to take ownership.** This means all the things outlined earlier—getting clear on what we want, working out how to get them, and then most importantly, communicating our needs. As a driven and motivated generation, we know the necessity of taking charge and leading the way with the things that we want in life—and our careers are no exception.

The career of a millennial is not what it used to be—with the departure from "traditional careers" reflected in many of their existing experiences. A diverse, multifaceted career portfolio, reflecting focus on experience, expansion, integration, and value add. For managers, understanding the drivers behind millennial careers, what they want, and where they're going is key to be able to support them in a way that isn't just meaningful but conducive to allowing them to become and achieve their goals and objective—including their current workplace, meaning a reciprocity of retention and giving back.

CHAPTER 4

Millennials in the Workplace

Generational Diversity and Management

The Challenge

It's not uncommon to hear workplaces and managers expressing difficulties when it comes to hiring, inspiring, training, and retaining quality employees—especially millennials. In fact, the "how to manage millennials" challenge for some workplaces has become all too elusive. Resignation to the beliefs and perceptions that millennials are "impossible to manage" or "impossible to retain" is oftentimes the easiest response.

The issue with this "resigning to the fact" is the problems that it is causing in many workplaces: (1) biased approaches toward management, which project attitudes and behavior of managers that translate to millennials in a less than ideal light; (2) power struggles between managers and millennials, which cause millennials to resist and push back (e.g., "You need to do as I say" met with "Don't tell me what to do."); (3) intergenerational conflict that extends more broadly between manager and millennial, impacting workplace culture; (4) performance issues, oftentimes via disengagement of millennials; and (5) high turnover rates and inability to retain millennial talent.

However, the perception that may exist around the difficulties in how to manage is arguably due to a lack of understanding versus the reality. **Part of the challenge of how to manage millennials effectively is hindered by outdated beliefs and stereotypes that exist.** Which in turn automatically limit the willingness that is needed to better understand this generation; in particular, how to get the best out of them.

The Why

Management problems infiltrate workplaces all around the world. Building a workplace that supports millennials is an area of focus that has gained significant attention in recent times for obvious reasons. And while the managing millennials challenge appears complex, at the end of the day, the onus is workplaces; more specifically managers—as the "who is responsible" points largely, back to them.

Managers have significant influence within a workplace, especially how an employee feels about their job. It is the manager who is responsible for ensuring that people know what work needs to be done, translates how this work contributes to the wider vision (i.e., the "why"), and supports their day to day and future career needs. This is why good management matters; the longevity of solid performance, supportive cultures, and retention of good people rely on this. For millennials, it's not an exception: they want great managers.

Key for managers is **understanding how millennials think, what they want, and what they need from their managers** to create an opportunity to better manage both their strengths and their weaknesses. For managers, part of understanding requires looking equally at "what not to do" and where the impact is being felt as much as it is on learning the "how to."

Generational Diversity

Not understanding the role of generational diversity and intergenerational challenges can present as problematic. Generational diversity can be considered as the "hum" in the background of most workplaces: silent unless it's called out due to specific problems or issues. Generational diversity is the concept of having a wide range of generations in the workforce, with each of those generations bringing different viewpoints and perspectives. Not understanding the nuisances of this in the workplace presents itself through unintended consequences: disengagement, poor performance or, worst case, loss of millennial talent. For managers, this means recognizing that millennials have different wants and needs to older generations and therefore **require a different style of management.**

Subscribing to Stereotypes

Millennials aren't naive: They know that workplaces can adopt a cynical and judgmental attitude when it comes to their lifestyle and attitude, and that they often come with "labels." What is unhelpful is when managers "buy into" or "subscribe" to these stereotypes or adopt preconceived notions about millennials (including how they should be managed). This also includes mistaking ambition with entitlement. While ambitious millennials are more likely to speak confidently about subjects where they may not have the level of experience or knowledge as older colleagues, it's not because they intend to sound presumptuous but more to do with eagerness and desire. Such approaches or biased perceptions risk breeding contempt and cynicism among millennials. Rather, what millennials need from managers is for them to **treat them on face value, fairly, and without bias.**

Misunderstand Millennial Motivators

There's a theory that knowing what you don't want is as important as knowing what you do want. This same principle applies and is most relevant in cases where managers don't understand (or misunderstand) the "why," desire, and motivators of millennials. While the "how to" will be covered later in this chapter, what is important to examine are some of the management-specific tensions that both managers and millennials face.

Arguably, best practice management requires an ability to understand what motivates people—because those managers who aren't fully engaged with teams won't (and can't) drive outcomes and performance. This applies even more critically to millennials. **Not understanding what motivates them means managers can't get the best out of them.** Unfortunately, there are many managers who are not only unaware but also misinformed; rather than seeing millennials as impact-motivated, misperceive millennials to care more about extraneous perks or benefits that come with a job—which outdated beliefs typically align with traditional ways of working. Impact-driven millennials instead care about the impact of their work—and to the degree that they are able to overlook individual success for the greater good.[1]

---

[1] T. Foster. 2017. *Multigenerational Impacts on the Workplace* (Bentley University: Gloria Cordes Larson Center for Women and Business (CWB)).

Not Enough Investment in Professional Development

Tied closely with career exploration and progression is the need for professional development—something that most millennials consider a must. The need for **growth and expansion are core to their values**, and statistics support that.[2] When managers don't understand the criticality of this need for professional growth and development, then they can't provide the opportunities to support millennials. Inadvertently creating a "red flag" for engagement and retention.

Not Enough Feedback

Many workplaces use performance reviews as a means of communicating feedback to people. Often this takes place every 6 to 12 months. While it might feel like an adequate approach, millennials need more; the gap is simply too long. **Millennials are goal-oriented and prefer continuous actionable feedback.** They want to ensure that they are doing the right thing and making progress toward their goals—which links strongly to the reward stimulus-response. While arguably there is a fine line between constant praise acting as a quasi-validation to their own anxiety-induced internal perfection toward the standards of their own performance, it is generally because they care about development.

Unclear Expectations

One of the common challenges and complaints of managers is that millennials have too great of expectations, which often translates into perceived entitlement at work. However, what is oftentimes missed as part of the onboarding experience (which isn't just about millennials) is the establishment of what those expectations are. And **millennials need clearly defined expectations**, which work in conjunction with their goal setting.

Limited Flexibility

Flexibility is one of the most important values to millennials. This requirement was already an ongoing agenda item before the pandemic

---

[2] *How Millennials Want to Work and Live.* 2016. Gallup Inc., US. www.gallup.com/workplace/238073/millennials-work-live.

emphasized the need for workplaces to adopt new ways of working. For millennials, flexibility encompasses hours, location, and preferences (vis-à-vis priorities and deliverables). The work life integration that millennials strive to achieve means that **work is just another element to their lives** rather than a separate component. This is where the failing of managers can occur—not understanding the holistic approach founded on a different view of the role of jobs and careers for this generation.

Not Enough Room for Failure

Given we exist in a success-driven society, it may sound nonsensical to talk about the role of failure. There is an important place for it, although one that many workplaces are missing. It's relevance to millennials, an important tool to overcome the fact **they weren't set up to experience what "failure" might look or feel like** (by their parents) and the offset of technology. From a workplace perspective, the "unable to fail" mentality has presented challenges: millennials not showing enough initiative, can't (or won't) make decisions, and need to ask for guidance (permission) on everything—prompting much frustration from managers.

While good managers know that all employees, regardless of generation, bring their own challenges, value, and experience to the workplace, millennials present a unique set. Which means when it comes to understanding what millennials want and need out of their manager, **workplaces need to invest an extra level of detail.** It's only then can workplaces truly accommodate and support their millennials teams—and get the best out of them.

Management Best Practices

What Millennials Want

There isn't a shortage of information on what it means to manage, let alone how to be a good manager. However, despite the available content on what these practices and principles are, there are still significant ways to go—especially when it comes to managing millennials. Boiled down into simple terms, good management practices are designed to get the best out of employees: to maximize their potential and draw on unique skills that ultimately lead to improved performance.

When it comes to management, workplaces vary in quality. From the manager who has high-performing teams to the manager getting mediocre performance because of "blanket style management"; or to the uneducated manager who doesn't have the knowledge or skills (usually because workplaces won't invest), which results in poor-performing teams. Statistics already indicate that poor management is one of the top reasons employees quit a job: in fact, two out of five employees are more likely to leave a job due to poor managers. When it comes to millennials, however, it doubles (make that 80 percent).[3]

Managing well is not simply about understanding what best practice techniques are—we know that theory and practice are two different sides of the coin. It's about the **application of those practices in a way that is effective and meaningful** to the individual.

Understanding *exactly* what it is that millennials want from their managers isn't often a conversation that's aired in workplaces. This isn't necessarily because it's off limits, but more because workplaces aren't necessarily aware of the value behind asking this question. Instead, shifting the attention from the "human" ask to the practical approach, which can sometimes be counterintuitive and unintentionally problematic. Admittedly, while some managers may feel like it's a can of worms to be opened—and move in the opposite direction—the simple fact is that increased awareness can only lead to progress. This isn't to say that millennials will always present with a straightforward response—they can be complex after all—but understanding their perspective and needs is important.

What millennials want from managers is more than just the best practice techniques. What's critical for millennials is **when managers can integrate best practice techniques with a human lens: starting with understanding who they are, the millennials**.

How to Support

Managing millennials requires workplaces to change or modify their management style. And while this may cause discomfort for older

[3] Goodhire. 2022. *Horrible Bosses: Are American Workers Quitting Their Jobs or Quitting Their Managers?* www.goodhire.com/resources/articles/horrible-bosses-survey/.

generations who are used to other ways of working and types of management, millennials are different and require a different approach. Accommodating their unique skills, values, and attitudes isn't just necessary as we are becoming a millennial-centric world, but doing it well means workplace benefits: improved morale, decreased turnover, and better engagement.

What millennials want from their managers is to adopt an **approach that resonates with them**—which includes the human element and style. Understanding the persona, or "type of manager" that millennials prefer, is therefore key.

Character

More Like a Leader, Less Like a Manager

Leadership and management are not the same thing, albeit they are often used interchangeably. The simplest way to differentiate is: leaders have people who follow them, while managers have people who work for them. To get the best out of people, workplaces need both: a strong leader and manager. However, not all leaders are (or can) managers and not all managers are (good) leaders. But you can strike luck and have a person be effective at both.

When it comes to millennials, **what they desire is a leadership-type approach.** They want a relationship with their manager that is coaching- and mentoring-oriented, rather than authoritarian or hierarchical. Part of their nature is a willingness to connect on a personal level, so they can build trust and mutual respect. And while it might feel a touch paradoxical—the fact they need structure, support, and firm decision making, yet at the same time crave the relational and somewhat Emotional intelligence (EQ) connection—it isn't overly complicated. More of a "firm resolve, gentle approach" position.

Open-Minded

One of the mutual grievances for millennials and their managers is the "pay your dues" mentality, which acts as a contentious point within workplace relationships. While acknowledging older generations entered the workforce when work and life were perhaps separate and distinct—vis-à-vis strong separation between the two—this type of workplace arrangement isn't something millennials necessarily warm to. Not least because of their broader values-based approach to integration but because of the need for stimulation and progress—which isn't always accommodated by waiting in a position to "pass time" simply for the sake of it.

Millennials are natural-born innovators, and sitting in stagnant roles introduces boredom and stagnation—neither of which is conducive to performance. They are somewhat impatient for advancement opportunities—but not to be confused with the traditional corporate ladder (which has become largely outdated). This also extends to the idea of seniority taking precedence over innovative ideas that come from millennials. Every new generation has entered the workplace to optimize antiquated processes passed down to them by the generation. However, there are still many instances of workplaces getting stuck in the past and not conducting proper analysis into future trends.

What millennials want is a workplace and manager who **offer and support a democratized environment that values collective knowledge, ideas, and the quality of work.** And with that means a step away from the traditional approach.

Shared or Respected Value

Openness, honesty, and transparency are core values of millennials—and they expect the same from their workplace and managers. This approach to keeping lines of communication open and working in a way that promotes collaboration is incredibly important. And while some managers may find it unusual that millennials are eager to engage in frequent dialogue with them, it's a critical way to building trust.

Style

From a practical point of view, there are several techniques that support leveraging the best of millennial talent.

Understand Their "Why" and Intertwine This Purpose With Their Role

Engagement drives performance—and statistics continue to iterate this.[4] However, it's hard to engage people if managers don't understand what's important to their teams—which is why understanding the "why" matters. In addition, is the need to link this "why" or motivator back to their role, the vision of the organization, or, more broadly, humanity and the planet. **Millennials need a sense of purpose**. Making a difference and being of value are critical to this generation. Which is why the more they can both understand and see that what they are doing is directly linked to their own purpose, passion, or wider contribution to the world, will accelerate engagement and performance.

Set Clear Expectations and Ensure That Developmental Opportunities

Vague expectations—or the lack of—are a pressing cause of anxiety for millennials. What millennials need—and respect—is being given clear expectations and goals, coupled with flexibility on how they should go about achieving them. **Goals are important and act as an exceptional way to incentivize performance**. With an appetite for learning and development, millennials must have an opportunity to grow professionally. This also ties in with their notion of success—and whether it fits with the organization's culture. If it doesn't, they will swiftly move on. Providing opportunity is one of the easiest ways to gain buy-in. If millennials can see that something is going to provide new skills, add value to their lives, or simply make them better people, they'll dive in.

Provide Consistent Feedback

Millennials want feedback, encouragement, and support. They want to ensure that they are doing things correctly and giving their level best

---

[4] D. Carnegie. 2018. *Managers Matter: A Relationship-Centered Approach to Engagement.* www.dalecarnegie.com.

to provide value. But it's not just about the feedback, it's about how that feedback is delivered. And for millennials, they prefer this to be done in a way that resonates with how they are. The best way to do this is rather than identifying what isn't working up, is to first recognize what is working and build on that, weaving in areas of improvement. If done well, millennials will see the opportunity in development versus a perceived criticism and failure of their performance (and, in turn, save a lot of anxiety and stress). **Millennials also like their efforts to be appreciated and rewarded.** Whether in time, flexibility, money, or a simple thank you, showing recognition and appreciation as part of this feedback will go a long way.

Give Millennials Autonomy, Flexibility, and the Balance
They Require to Be Their Best Selves

Millennials want autonomy, not micro-management. They want to have independence over what they do, when they do it, how they do it, and who they do it with. As a generation who live and breathe flexibility and adaptability in day to day life, they want to feel like they're trusted to manage their own time and energy. **They view workplaces that offer flexibility as more modern and in tune with their life and needs**—and gravitate strongly to workplaces that can offer this. And while for some industries, it might not be practical to let employees work from home most of the time, being open-minded to alternative working models (including a mindset shift of outputs versus time spent) is worth having the conversation about.

Foster a Sense of Team and Community

Millennials' **sense of community matters,** and they oftentimes prefer to work as a team. They value work friendships and being part of a positive, fun culture. In fact, an International Business Machines Corporation (IBM) workforce study conducted in 2015 outlined that almost 60 percent of millennials felt that they made better decisions when receiving input from other sources. This ties in with their conditioned upbringing of social media and networking. For managers, **ensuring that elements of collaboration and team building exist frequently is important.**

Provide Tools and Technology

One of the biggest grievances millennials have when it comes to operations is working in workplaces that are behind modern-day times of using technology as a tool to increase effectiveness, productivity, and performance. Having to work under the constraints of outdated processes or systems doesn't just limit their ability to perform but creates frustration. Managers need to be willing to **let millennials introduce new ideas on ways of doing things more efficiently** (process and technology) and give them an opportunity to "do what they do best": innovate, improve, and then deliver.

Encourage Permission to Fail

The best interests of millennials (agreed by all or not) would see an environment where they can fail without judgment. One of the ways managers can facilitate this is by encouraging a broader "culture" change that embraces a "permission to fail" mindset, where failure is celebrated for its ability to teach and provide learnings and for the opportunity to build collaboration among teams. **Encouraging millennials to make mistakes allows them to develop confidence**—not just in themselves but in their role in the workplace; for being in an environment that supports and nurtures their appetite to grow and evolve—including the introduction of innovation and ideas—flourishes commitment and engagement.

Consider Reverse Mentoring

One of the biggest challenges millennials face in management or leadership positions is usually the lack of experience. Limited experience means that dealing with staff and understanding the correct processes on how to manage can be difficult. However, learning from other colleagues who have had the experience, or other managers within a workplace, can be a valuable way of fast-tracking the learning curve. Reverse mentoring—or simply mentoring—can act as a powerful way of **transferring knowledge and skills that also supports a more cohesive and productive culture at work.**

Establishing rapport and understanding with millennials is not as insurmountable as some managers may think. All it takes is a decision and the willingness to learn. Doing it right can make all the difference in keeping performance and engagement high, retaining quality talent, and nurturing a flourishing high-performing culture.

For Millennials: How to Get What You Want

For us to be the best people we can be at work means **we must work with our managers**. It's a two-way street: and from a management point of view, there are things we do well and things that we can improve on. Most of this comes down to understanding the "gaps" that act as barriers to getting to where we want to be.

Understand Who We Are and What We Want

As the saying goes, "You don't know, what you don't know." And for millennials, that translates to: (1) if we don't understand how we prefer to be managed, we can't perform to the best of our ability; and (2) if we're managing other millennials, then face the risk of not getting the best out of them either. Understanding ourselves means we can better understand others (young, old, or otherwise).

Understand (or at Least Appreciate) Others

The dynamics of today's workplaces mean we have five generations of people working together. That's a lot of contrast and diversity—and equally, one of the reasons pain points exist. People are going to irritate you—and equally, you, them. We are human. However, key to being able to operate in a way that helps us move toward our goals is taking the time to appreciate the dynamics—which includes where your manager may be coming from, including the generational viewpoints and differences that might be operating in the background.

For those who are managing older colleagues (Boomers, Gen X: often referred to as "managing up"), there are two key areas that need particular focus: hierarchy and communication.

Approaches to Authority and Hierarchy.   Generations look at authority differently—and for millennials, we adopt an equal playing field position. However, just because we like it this way, doesn't mean our managers do. **We need to be mindful of our own behavior and the perception this might generate**—that is, interpreted as a lack of respect, defiant behavior, or a sense of entitlement. The same typically applies to supervision and management styles and the varying degrees to which generations appreciate supervision and feedback. We want feedback and value having a mentor, while older generations may be insulted by it. This is particularly important for millennials who are managing older colleagues.

Approaches to Communication.   We are a generation that has grown up in a world of technology, having a conversation online, or sending someone a text to ask for something is normal. But we need to remember that **our experience and preference regarding communication aren't necessarily the norm for others.** Conversation, phone calls, and IRL are still valid—and matter. We need to be conscious that our preference isn't always the most beneficial way of engaging with people.

The communication issue also ties in with our use of technology. While we're adept with online social networking, for some of us, this has come at a cost: our ability to develop interpersonal relationships with our colleagues. Some workplaces and sectors (e.g., health care) rely very much on interpersonal relationships and connections to get things done. A point of contention for workplaces, especially with the younger of our generation, is a perceived unwillingness or reservation to reach out to colleagues—including managers—to get things done.

Understand Where We Can Do Better

Show Initiative.   A reported pain point for managers is new hires (in particular) not showing enough initiative—expecting managers or colleagues to solve their problems rather than using their own resourcefulness to overcome obstacles. The offset of helicopter parenting and technology hasn't helped this—but we could support ourselves and managers by **taking the lead and reaching out to others more, to get things done.** Recognizing that it's ok to raise a suggestion, or to offer feedback without the "fear" of doing the wrong thing, or any accountability that comes with that.

Be More Decisive.   We know that being presented with too many options isn't a good thing. The overwhelm of choice can be a challenge, and one we experience in the workplace. This has resulted in pain points regarding decision making. Our managers and colleagues simply want us to **make an educated choice**, not sit in agony or take an age to make up our minds (even if all solutions presented appear as good as one another). While we know this stems from our "need to get it right" perfectionism traits, the downside is spending too long researching or laboring over the right thing to do causes unnecessary anxiety. If needed, "fake it until you make it," as there is a lot to be said in confidence. Make a decision and be comfortable with it.

Be Mindful of Expectations.   Admittedly, there are several of us who've been guilty of bringing that "unshakeable sense of self belief and entitlement attitude" to work—despite having only just set off on our career. While our level of self-assurance is commendable, it's unfortunately been perceived as arrogant by our peers. Instant gratification aside, **we must be mindful of being able to separate that pressing need for "now"** when it comes to our workplace and careers—and, in turn, what we expect from our managers. Sure, have that high level of drive, or the desire to be a leader, or to climb or embed yourself into whatever part of the workplace you want, but recognize that you're not going to cover five years' experience in six months. Key for us is also **considering other colleagues' values and experience**—especially those who've formed careers through years of service—and the loyalty and commitment that comes with that. This isn't to say we can't get what we want "at pace," but exercising patience and respect is helpful.

Don't Take Things Personally.   We are a passionate generation who—when we find something we connect with—invest our heart and soul into it. The offset of this means we may feel slightly more vulnerable at times. Which is why **not taking things personally** and remaining as objective (and unoffended) as possible is important. Especially when we find ourselves in uncomfortable situations or difficult conversations with managers or colleagues.

Find a Supportive Manager

While we don't always get to choose our managers, we can exercise judgment and determine if the existing arrangement is conducive for us to be our best selves. We know intuitively when we're in places that serve or hinder. Irrespective of whether we end up with a bad manager, we can do what we can to influence our workplace situations.

We have a responsibility in the relationship we create with our managers. Start by having a conversation; it's that simple. Don't assume that your manager knows what you want or need. And recognize that the feeling of being valued, isn't just about us—it's a human desire. If your manager becomes aware that you're needing a mentor, or specific support, they'll likely feel more valued in their roles. In fact, you might unintentionally support their own wants; creating a space for them to feel honored and appreciated.

If the situation isn't changeable (i.e., the manager isn't going anywhere), then find someone else who may be able to support your career needs. Whether that be another manager of a different team, a mentor, or simply a like-minded colleague—someone who can help you harbor your goals, help fulfill your "why," and provide the support and understanding that you need. Finding this person may make all the difference in shifting where you are right now to where you want to be. At the end of the day, taking control of our careers and jobs is up to us.

Millennials are an invaluable asset. They bring a fresh perspective, passion, and drive to succeed into their day to day lives in the workplace. If managers want to effectively manage millennials, it requires a different approach. One that might take time to adjust to, but one that is well worth the investment. For millennials, key to success with managers is to understand who they are in the context of their persona and background but to fundamentally play your part in co-creating the relationship you want.

CHAPTER 5

Millennials in the Workplace

Engage, Retain, Recruit

The Challenge

Millennials make up a significant part of the workforce. As a result, workplaces are beginning to come to realize the criticality of the need to pay more attention—and to listen—to the needs of their millennials if they are to get the best out of them.

Already, keeping employees engaged and attracting and retaining talent are some of the biggest challenges workplaces are already experiencing. Year in, year out, these issues continue to remain somewhat elusive. Arguably because workplaces haven't connected how these people-related issues are heavily correlated to success (i.e., bottom line) and in addition, failing to understand the "how to" resolve these challenges effectively. Furthermore, is that oftentimes workplaces overlook or misdirect investment into other business functions such as systems, processes, or technology. Areas of the workplace that—given the perceived "tangibility" or "obvious" nature—are given more weight.

More specifically, however, are the **engagement, retention, and attraction challenges associated with millennials**—who are one of the hardest generations to engage. Engagement perplexing many a manager and causing stress, given the "flight factor" of this generation—who are, admittedly, already looking forward and outward for opportunity, regardless of their engagement in current roles. But not just that, the reality of having to manage "real time" engagement and retention against a backdrop of statistics that suggest millennials are already twice as likely to leave a workplace than other generations.[1] It's a significant figure—and

---

[1] *How Millennials Want to Work and Live.* 2018. Gallup, Inc. US. www.gallup.com/workplace/238073/millennials-work-live.aspx.

amplified when you consider the cost factor (i.e., invested time, effort, and money into hiring or training, loss of potential, etc.).

However, it's beyond the tenure time limit that is causing the most discomfort. Instead, it's arguable the constant questions and scenarios that managers are finding themselves having to plan or find solutions for. Namely: "What do I have to do as a manager to keep my millennials motivated and enthused, on task and performing and producing quality outputs? And with all this, limit the amount of time I have think about it and exert effort into it, so I can feel less exhausted and not as if I'm constantly behind them."

Against the managerial (and personal) stress is the reality that indicates workplaces still don't have the answers. Not with statistics finding that only 29 percent of millennials are engaged at work, and that the majority (55 percent) are actively disengaged.[2] The result being a millennial departure from the workplace—which has been further complicated by the pandemic-inspired Great Resignation. A movement being led by millennial and Gen Z employees; one that signifies an alarmingly significant growth of job dissatisfaction among younger generations.

Big problem—especially considering that engagement impacts retention. And while engagement was seen as a safeguard to keeping millennials—a lynch pin existing between recruitment and retention—it's no longer simply engagement that's become critical. **With the absence of appetite to stay in unsuitable jobs or apply for jobs that millennials don't see as a "fit," the attraction issue—that is, how do we get millennials in our door—has become paramount to resolve.** And right now, it's a job seekers market, meaning there are more open positions than applicants. This means (millennial) job seekers have the upper hand rather than workplaces—placing more strain on the ability to source them. And for a generation who aren't shy of claiming their worth, and won't typically settle with mediocre, means that workplaces must go the extra mile to secure talent. With millennials now making up the majority of today's workforce—the "end to end" process from attraction, through to engagement, through to retention—is one that needs to be examined and given the attention that it requires.

---

[2] Ibid.

The Why

The "why" behind the engagement, retention, and recruitment issues that workplaces are experiencing isn't clear-cut (and not that it should be, given it involves people). However, when it comes to millennials, there are several factors workplaces need to understand that influence and impact these challenges. While those outlined could be argued to be applicable to all types of employees, those discussed at the top of the list for millennials—which means managers and workplaces need to understand these. Failing to understand the complexities will continue to cost workplaces—especially financially. In fact, if we look at the United States, the turnover rate of millennials is costing the U.S. economy $30.5 billion annually.[3]

Engagement

Little or Lack of Investment Into Engagement

The effort invested in addressing challenges of engagement—not just the establishment of an engagement plan but identifying (where needed) the root cause of how to manage staff disengagement—is few and far between. Arguably, some workplaces don't even understand the concept of "engagement." And while what works for one employee may not work for another, it's fair to say that there are consistencies with what employee engagement in the workplace means.

Usually defined as the level of involvement and enthusiasm of people in their work and workplace, engagement is oftentimes taken for granted. And with "taken for granted," it means mostly around the inability of workplaces to understand the correlation between levels of engagement and performance. How the ups and downs translate across the workplace and impact the bottom line.

When engagement is working well, workplaces find themselves with people who have a sense of purpose, are committed, performing well, work collaboratively, have positive attitudes, and an openness to

---

[3] Bureau of Labor Statistics. 2020. cited in *The Truth About Millennial Turnover*, Recruiting.com, US. www.recruiting.com/blog/the-truth-about-millennial-turnover/.

communicate. When it's not working well, then it flips all the afore-mentioned around: **poor performance, low morale, less focus, risks to retention, and financial costs (tangible and nontangible).** And argu-ably, while this isn't just a millennial-specific issue, the level of impact felt vis-à-vis the consequences on performance and productivity is almost guaranteed to manifest itself most significantly within this generation. Translating into risk of significant declines in workplace productivity and the loss of quality millennial talent.

And this scenario—both the risk of it, and its manifestation—is being played out across workplaces all around the world. Situations that can be managed and risks that can be mitigated, with the right education, awareness, and approach.

A One-Size-Fits-All Model Approach

It's not uncommon for workplaces to assume that all employees want the same thing and that keeping them engaged can be done through a "blan-ket approach." Coupled with this is the mistaken expectation that having loyal and dedicated employees, without the need to invest, is a given. However, if there is no reciprocal investment in workplace relationships, then it results in dissatisfaction. Specifically for millennials, there has been (and is) a growing percentage who are feeling unsupported and dissatis-fied (cue the Great Resignation).

Retention

Poor Management

Arguably, there is **no relationship in the workplace more powerful than the one between managers and their employees.** And for mil-lennials, this rings true. The biggest problem that workplaces are being presented with are managers who are poorly trained and don't know how to manage, aren't skilled enough and can't get the best out of their people, or are simply poor managers because of their own attitude or behavioral issues (e.g., the "sink or swim approach"). The latter being the biggest problem for workplaces and by far the most toxic. In fact, statistics paint a very dire picture of the actuality. Not just in how employees feel about their managers but the financial cost and loss of hundreds of billions (the United States).[4]

Values and Needs Mismatch

Although on the one hand, the needs of millennials are clear, some workplaces still struggle to meet these needs and, in turn, are unable to attract millennials to their workplace. Despite the stereotypes, especially those that surround the misconception that millennials aren't interested in work, the ability (or inability) to attract and retain quality talent has nothing to do with these perceived "don't want to work" or "lazy" myths. In fact, it's the opposite: millennials want more out of life. They don't live to work or feel a need to subscribe to "the grind of 9-5" that previous generations may be used to. They live through an experiential lens, where meaning matters and what they do with their career and jobs matters.

This **values-based approach and desire differ dramatically from what previous generations wanted**. And those in Human Resources in charge of recruitment, or managers trying to retain, fail to understand and operate at a mismatch.

The Mental Health Agenda

With burnout on the rise, the world has progressively been seeing more of the millennial generation leave their jobs. The pandemic brought the issue of burnout to the forefront of many workplaces—in addition to several other compounding and related factors. And while it might feel counterintuitive to think that this period exacerbated the burnout factor, there were several factors at play.

First, the **inability to separate personal and professional lives**. This exacerbated the "switched on" factor that millennials were already experiencing and in turn the adverse impacts to mental health. Second, many

---

[4] Society for Human Resource Management. 2020. cited in *Survey: 84 Percent of U.S. Workers Blame Bad Managers for Creating Unnecessary Stress.* www.shrm.org/about-shrm/press-room/press-releases/pages/survey-84-percent-of-us-workers-blame-bad-managers-for-creating-unnecessary-stress-.aspx.

workplaces didn't cope well with the change—leaving many feeling like they had little or, in some cases, no support. This has left many millennials questioning their workplaces' investment and care factor for their well-being. Third, opportunity came to a halt—leaving many millennials feeling irritated and "stuck."

For millennials, the most fundamental questions this challenged them to ask themselves were not only the reassessment of workplaces and how they responded but their own lives and whether the ways of working that once saw them move to a pathway of stress, workload burdens and depletion to well-being, was still worth it. The answer, for many—and reflected through the Great Resignation—was "no." A realization among this generation that the old ways of working were not conducive to supporting their well-being and that their **mental health and, in turn, workplaces that support culture of well-being were now a high priority.**

Diversity, Equality, and Inclusion

Recent years have seen the rise of matters relating to DEI (EDI) become pressing priorities. More recently, DEI has evolved to include a focus on justice (JEDI—justice, equality, diversity, and inclusion), which looks at breaking down the barriers created by events. From LGBTIQ+ to BLM to MeToo movement, the world is undeniably becoming more inclusive. And while these matters affect the world at large, the actions of **advocating, supporting, and encouraging these types of social change are hugely important to millennials.** Understanding that they are not immune to the world around them, and with great emphasis on values that support equality in all matters, the continuation of a world that is forward thinking and forward moving will continue. And arguably, largely, with the leadership of millennials as they move into positions of power.

Recruitment

The Changing Nature of Work and the Workplace

Over the last few decades, the world has seen a shift in not just the values being brought in by millennials that governs what work means, but the nature of work—that is, the workplace, what this looks like and how work is done—has also changed. While technology has been a huge proponent for changing the shape of the traditional workplace and the types of jobs being offered, there are several other key changes.

The growth of the Gig Economy. The Gig Economy refers to the segment of the workforce involved in freelance, contractual, or part-time work instead of the typical 9 to 5. While not new, it has become increasingly popular among the younger generation over the years. With the pandemic interrupting and disrupting business ways of working, this type of working gained popularity.

There are several factors which have influenced the shift from traditional work to the Gig Economy. First is the shift of preference and new values entering the workplace—arguably influenced millennials. That being, the 9 to 5 job that was once considered the "dream job" is no longer the case. In fact, this type of **traditional working has lost appeal**, given that such roles typically don't afford flexibility that most younger generations yearn for. And for those who hadn't yet had a taste of what different looks like—that is, not being stuck in an office for eight hours a day—the pandemic opened that door. Second is the **influential factors of technology and the Internet**. This has afforded both flexibility and the alleviation of any geographical boundaries, with people able to work with laptops from anywhere in the world. In turn, allowing many people to create new lifestyles that shift the "live life to work" to a more integrated fashion where life and travel can be experienced at the same time as work—that is, digital norms. And it's this third reason they **want to live more harmonious and connected lives** that is perhaps the most powerful.

The Great Resignation. Since the pandemic hit, record numbers of millennials have left their jobs. Reasons are varied but include lack of support from management, burnout, stress, a mismatch in values, and simple epiphanies about their life choices. Record numbers of people relying on government benefits and their overly stringent rules about earning extra income also removed incentives to undertake "lower level" casual employment.

While many employees were forced into lockdown for extended periods of time and noncritical workers were enjoying the novelty of working from home, something happened. With the pandemic forcing workplaces to be more flexible and innovative than most thought possible, which included leveraging the benefits of technology and the realization that remote working was entirely feasible and not a "new age concept" (albeit industry-specific), it embarked **not just a contagion of quitting, but a shift in mindset from "traditional" to "new."** And subsequently, a realization that this "trend" and demands of improved ways of working (with a plea from millennials to "not going back") won't be going away.

Is it just a millennial thing? Well, yes and no. Many people began to wonder whether they really needed to be in the office, and ever wanted to be again. And while Boomers and Gen X have felt the benefit—and some will advocate these ways moving forward—for millennials, this period, this revolution of sorts, is being felt and leaving a mark globally.

Management Best Practices

What Millennials Want

To attract the best talent, or retain and unlock the potential of existing, requires an **approach that looks at both the individual and environment.** While emphasis has been given to the criticality of understanding the millennial "person" as a value-based individual, the next "iteration" is to expand that into the environment. Putting on the hat of a millennial and asking yourself "Knowing what I know about millennials, what type of workplace would I want to be part of? And what type of workplace would inspire me to do the best I can and allow me to thrive?"

Irrespective of the individual wants that millennials have, there are a generalized set of requirements—or criteria—that almost all would agree to. **Requirements that are pertinent to the ability to attract, retain, and engage key talent.** Requirements which don't operate as an either-or but as a must-have. And requirements which, while at face value may look like separate entities, are deeply entrenched and connected.

In addition to the values and individual needs that managers must understand is more broadly the culture which fosters these. And for many millennials, this culture—the environment of a workplace and how it encompasses, inspires, nurtures, and accepts—is critical. Millennials want to be part of workplaces they feel part of and **to be able to bring their whole selves to work.** They want to work for workplaces that care about their individual needs and provide supportive conditions that allow them to work in a way where they feel they are doing the best they can, are able to strive for growth, and be of value and service.

Culture

Workplace culture can be defined as an accumulation of leadership, values, beliefs, attitudes, and a set of behavior which forms the environment. It also incorporates interpersonal relationships and demographics. For millennials, **a culture of well-being**—one that supports people to achieve balance and a positive state of health (physically, emotionally, and mentally) and is inclusive and respectful—is critical. Such support and prioritization are more than what appears on the surface; it's deeply connected to performance. In fact, research shows that well-being and performance are strongly correlated. Low rates of well-being correlate with low rates of performance: burnout, retention issues, and lack of engagement are all symptoms of an underlying problem within a workplace's culture.

Despite the already existing need for better workplace cultures, the pandemic forced the criticality of this to the surface—not least because of the drastic shift in ways of working and its effects on engagement, performance, and mental health.

Workplace well-being and the prioritization of mental health have become emphasized criteria for millennials. Not only because this generation is suffering burnout and arguably tired of the constant berating of their mental health in workplaces that don't listen, but because they realize their own responsibility in taking care of their selves. That mental health, burnout, and stress can't be contained to a box.

In addition, is their willingness to start challenging workplaces on removing barriers, stigma, and behavior of managers who downplay or demonstrate a disregard for the importance of well-being. (For example, telling millennials the reason they're burnt out is because they can't manage their personal life.)

A culture of well-being is one of the most **critical factors millennials consider** when it comes to remaining in a workplace. And while JEDI and DEI (EDI) have been raised, the point must be emphasized that these elements are part of the culture and of significant weight. If workplaces don't offer support or services that adequately address these concerns, they will leave. The same applies for attraction: millennials are attracted to workplaces where focus and emphasis is on well-being; and where mental health is honored.

The cost of mental health is beginning to fall heavily on the shoulders of workplaces, especially as our younger workforce continues to grow, meaning there is now a critical obligation for workplaces to provide a conducive culture which includes adequate mental health support.

Trust

While a common-sense mindset would agree that trust forms the basis of all relationships, some workplaces are yet to fully appreciate the criticality of this. Trust is a necessity for performance. Without trust, workplaces are at risk of declines in all areas of growth. Workplaces must recognize that millennials hold trust as a core value—and that this is both the starting point for their relationship and what they expect ongoing.

Millennials benefit and are most appreciative of workplace that make trust an explicit objective; those that are clear about taking a proactive, transparent approach to matters that affect each of us as humans (and in turn our performance). This includes having more meaningful conversations, adopting an open and transparent philosophy, ensuring that morals and values are adhered to, committing to word, ensuring decisions are made from an ethical lens, and inspiring and motivating through action are key.

Belonging

How valued and supported people feel is almost always translated into how productive they are. For millennials, being valued directly translates into a sense of belonging and worth—which is critical for engagement. **Millennials appreciate a space where they can contribute to shared objectives, express feedback, input their ideas, and share experiences.** Fostering accountability is also important—not just for managers, but for millennials as part of their own actions in contributing to an environment which supports mental health and well-being.

Collaboration

Cohesive, high performing, happy millennial teams provide huge rewards. And collaboration is key for this. Not just within teams, but this also includes relationships with leaders. Millennials want to know that reciprocity exists—which is a departure from traditional structures that offer top-down approaches to management and leadership. **"At level thinking" fosters feelings of mutuality and respect**, which by default enhances collaboration.

Diverse and Inclusive

Developing a **culture that values justice, equality, inclusivity, and diversity is a must.** With progressive mindsets and equality-driven attitudes, millennials want to be working for workplaces that are tolerant and sensitive to the needs of their people. Whether it's refraining from using gender-specific pronouns, recognizing religious occasions, nurturing mental health, acknowledging systemic disadvantages, or providing more accessibility for people who are unable to work in a traditional office environment via remote working, there are simple ways to show you care—and in turn, a place that millennials want to be part of.

As a generation who are huge advocates for matters of diversity—and are confident to speak out—it's an area that workplaces can leverage from their millennials. Offering millennials an opportunity to focus on issues that matter—whether that be as a voice and/or activism responsibilities or developing or overseeing workplace projects that focus on JEDI or DEI—is an incentive to not just create change but act as an incentive.

Sustainability and Social Responsibility

Millennials are committed to making a social and sustainable impact, so much so that research suggests they are more attracted to making a positive impact in society and communities than starting a family.[5] With an increased level of awareness about issues affecting humanity and the planet, millennials are more willing to act than perhaps older generations. From a workplace perspective, this means that unless sustainability or cause is on the corporate agenda, and there is activity occurring—then attracting quality millennial talent will be a challenge.

How to Support

From attracting and retaining staff to changing culture and employee attitudes, improving leadership and management behavior or general workforce performance, most workplaces are not shy of the need to make improvements to these areas of the business.

Engagement

How to get the best millennials—and the best out of them—requires a multipronged approach. There are several elements that need to be considered and to best demonstrate these, a car analogy can be used.

A car's performance and the outcome of a journey are dependent on: (1) the driver (skill); (2) quality or type of fuel (feedback); (3) conditions such as the weather and road surface (environment); (4) signposts or map (direction); and (5) a destination (goal). When one of these elements is removed, reduced, or simply isn't operating as it should, the impacts are felt on both the performance and journey.

To get the best out of millennials, requires a multicomponent system approach: (1) understanding the millennial and their skills (including strength and weakness), (2) feedback on performance, (3) a culture and environment that support their performances, (4) the right structure and direction from managers, and (5) an end goal that motivates them.

---

[5] Deloitte Insights. 2019. *The Deloitte Global Millennial Survey 2019.*

Understand Millennial Values

Workplaces that can understand and nurture what millennials value are able to build a progressive culture of those who are both comfortable and engaged. This also extends to showing how they, as unique individuals, with their skills and experience, are **adding value or making a difference**. It doesn't have to be huge, but enough for them to feel that it's more than a job that they're getting paid for.

Opportunities for Growth

While salary and benefits are important for millennials, what they care most about is the ability to learn and grow as a professional and an individual. Learning, development, and growth are hugely important, and millennials won't remain in a job that's boring, mundane, or has no room for growth or career development. Millennials have a yearning for responsibility and opportunity. **They want opportunities that allow them to flourish.** For example, moving around the office, trying new roles, acting up, or promotional opportunities. They want to feel valued and assured that their career progression and wants can be fulfilled—regardless of how long that tenure is within a company.

The identification of this from the outset—that is, when new hires are recruited—is becoming increasingly important as many millennials are making sure that even at interview stage, they are asking the questions of interviewing officers of what progression or development opportunities exist.

Feedback, Positivity, and Recognition

Feedback matters to millennials—and even though they can continue to perform well without it, it makes a huge difference. This feedback isn't just about how they are performing as individuals but also their thoughts on specific matters. And while some strong-willed millennials will provide unsolicited feedback, opening a space for them where they feel their ideas and thoughts are actively welcomed—and they are encouraged to share—is critical for engagement.

Modern, Flexible, and Adaptable Environment

Adaptation to new ways of working—and a willingness to adapt to the shifts in millennial work culture—are a must. For workplaces and older colleagues, this means re-adjusting views or beliefs that are grounded in the idea of seniority taking precedence over innovative ideas that may come from millennials. **Antiquated processes don't work for millennials,** and those workplaces that are stuck or are unwilling to move ahead won't engage (or will attract or retain top-tier millennial talent). One only needs to look at the world's forward-thinking, most profitable companies to understand the criticality of progressive mindsets and the adoption of processes and ways of working that optimize business.

Any workplace that doesn't offer flexibility will be hard pressed to keep millennials engaged (and attract). While the pandemic offered many workplaces a "taster" of remote ways of working, millennials are unlikely to remain in workplaces where this isn't offered (full time or hybrid). Flexibility isn't just important to millennials, it's a factor that can potentially make or break their decision to remain with a workplace. While industry-specific limitations to remote ways of working will exist, allowing millennials to manage activities, such as travel, parenting, and spending time with family and friends while holding down a full-time job is important.

Finally, when it comes to conditions, **millennials want to maximize everything**; drip-feeding any work or employment condition doesn't typically sit well. If needed, offer more appealing conditions—whether that be splitting work into different types of opportunities, max existing opportunities, better pay, or more flexibility. These also act as additional incentives for performance.

Direction

Good management and leadership matters. This includes both how they are managed (with preference for mentor style) and who the manager is (with preference for role models). **Millennials want to be working with workplaces where their leaders "walk the talk" and lead by example.** For millennials who are ambitious, motivated, and wanting to make a difference, this can act as a powerful point of engagement vis-à-vis an influential type of relationship and something that managers can leverage.

Goals

Millennials want to be set up for success, and key to that is goals. To do this, managers should tap into millennials' intrinsic desire for personal fulfillment and a sense of purpose.

Retention

No workplace wants to experience high turnover rates—and managing this problem is complex because of a varying number of factors contributing. For millennials, there are several factors. For some, there are the "obvious reasons" that talent leaves: poor managers, bored, no career progress—quite simply jobs that don't provide what they want. The second is the experience factor and how they feel they fit with the culture. And finally, is whether they feel that they and the company are making a difference.

Key for managers is **what they can provide in terms of progression and environment** to maximize what they can get out of their millennials while in post. And in fact, providing them with the right environment or opportunities for development might even get them to stay longer.

Leadership and Management

Improving employee–manager relationships should be a key priority for workplaces. This starts with fostering a solid relationship (that is personable) between millennials and their managers.

Culture and Experience

One of the biggest challenges organizations have found is integrating millennials into a "pre-established" Boomer and Gen X culture. Workplaces that have been willing and able to adapt to a new generation and integrate different attitudes, behaviors, and ideas have been able to produce cultures of high performance. For some workplaces, however, the contrast has produced intergenerational conflicts and tensions, and in turn, impacted performance and retention. Surprisingly, the **nuisances that exist with intergenerational differences**—including the causes and reasoning—are still an area that workplaces are not sufficiently aware and educated about. Just like other matters of diversity, managers should promote awareness to harmonize workplace relationships, reduce intergenerational bias and conflict, and build collaboration cultures.

From an experiential point of view, a good reputation as a place to work and word of mouth are some of the best and easiest ways to attract and retain millennial talent. While the culture of a workplace can be impacted by various factors, those critical to millennials are centered around **diversity, leadership, management, and well-being**. And arguably, may become even more so, especially with matters surrounding JEDI and DEI (EDI).

In addition, millennials aren't tolerant of subpar experiences—so a poor recruitment process or having bad managers will very much influence their want to stay with a company. And while they're willing and open to talk through most problems or challenges (if given the opportunity), they are also aware of their value. Which means they are reluctant to stay and/or continue to experience situations/people that aren't serving them, or their careers, well.

Progression

If you are hiring casual millennials, it's likely your workplace is a steppingstone to something else. And while it costs workplaces to keep replacing millennials, managers would benefit from thinking about what they could offer to **incentivize them to stay** (at least longer). For example, can you create roles with more responsibility that employees can work their way up to? Can they potentially become full-time? What opportunities for learning and upskilling can you offer that provide a partnership?

Impact

Managers need to be able to clearly articulate the wider vision of the workplace and how their millennials are part of that. Millennials will gravitate to workplaces that have clear objectives which support their own career pathways, professional development, and align with their impact orientation values. They are **strongly biased toward working with workplaces that are making an impact**, leaving a legacy, or giving back to the planet in some way. So much so that they will choose to work with values-aligned workplaces over money—which means that workplaces must work harder to sell themselves if they want quality talent. Money isn't the leverage—it's the cause. And this cause-oriented career is something that millennials will actively seek out. So much so that they will actively assess—and reassess—their positions and contributions (professional and personal) to ensure they are aligned.

Recruitment

With trends like the Great Resignation occurring, and rates of unemployment high, there's been a balance of power shift to the hands of younger generations. What this means for workplaces is there is now greater importance and pressure in some respects to focus on the company marketing or sales pitch.

Vision, Mission, and "Why"

Attracting quality talent is no different from selling a product. And that product is the organization. For a generation who is used to scaling reviews, looking at options, and making informed decisions, this salability—and what the workplace offers—matters. And key to this is honesty and transparency in this messaging.

Attraction starts with the why: why your workplaces do what it does, and then the what and how this happens. Oftentimes workplaces overlook the importance of how **a well-thought-out vision and/or mission helps attract quality talent**. The heart of your business is your "why." It is the why you do what we do. This isn't to be confused with the "what." The "what" can be easily defined—it is what most businesses focus on when they market to the world. It is the product, or service. But if I were to ask you the question, why does your workplace (or you) do what you do, could you answer it as easily?

To grow, to be successful, workplaces need to understand why they do what they do. This 'why' is fundamentally linked to values, and it is these values—the 'heart'—that shape the way workplaces do business and ultimately lead to success. This why informs language, marketing, and, ultimately, adds credibility to workplaces; it builds better cultures and helps motivate employees—which is particularly important for millennials where finding purpose and a "why" is a critical part of their lives; it helps inform decision making in the best interests of the workplace by aligning with your core values. To attract and gain buy-in from millennials, making the values of the workplace personable is also important. If a review of values is needed, then do so with your teams: discuss and create them together. **Shared vision and values make for unification**—and a very attractive workplace to be part of.

Transferable Skills and Personality

One theory to recruiting is "hire for attitude, train for skills."[6] It's not hard to see why people who have the right attitude and willingness are more desirable than someone with the right skills and wrong attitude. Every single millennial who is bright and eager to work is worth 10 employees who don't really want to be there. When recruiting millennials, **look for those who are intuitively competent.** They will quickly add value when they show they can do more than just what you hired them for—and offering a space to do so supports long-term engagement.

For Millennials: How to Get What You Want

Whether you currently love or loathe the job you're in, there's never been a better time to check in and ask yourself some intentional questions, like "Is what I'm doing what I want to be doing?" and "Do I feel fulfilled?" If the answer is "no," then you need to be thinking about the "why." Is it because you've ended up in a career that you didn't want? Or perhaps you're feeling misunderstood in the workplace and experiencing intergenerational tensions? Are you about to hit the 12-month anniversary and feeling this level of commitment is weighing you down? Or is it simply because you have no idea what you want to do and the job you're in (or have been in) just doesn't feel right?

Regardless of the answer, the most important thing we need to be contemplating is the solution. Putting aside the fact that there may be

---

[6] Originally attributed to Herb Kelleher, co-founder of U.S.-based Southwest Airlines.

many of us who have quit—or are on the verge—there are things we can do to mitigate some of the tensions.

Decide What Matters

When it comes to selecting the workplace for us, we need to first **get clear on what type of workplace we want to be working for and why**. It might be as simple as the organization offers a great career progression, or that it's making huge inroads into sustainable causes, but without knowing what's important to us means we're at risk of selecting workplaces that won't fulfill our needs. Of course, experimenting through trial and error is encouraged—and it helps with the failure complex—but getting clear on what matters to you in the workplace is key for fulfillment.

Use Your Values to Guide Decisions

Our values guide us and play a key role in our decision making. When searching for a job, or a specific type of workplace, or being interviewed, it's critical to draw on those things that matter (e.g., partnership, collaboration, or teamwork). Interviews should be as much about us finding the right fit and asking questions of our prospective employer (or client) as it is for the potential employer. Which means, **there's onus on you to research, prepare, and ask the right questions** to ensure that the workplace you may be stepping into is the one for you.

Communicate (and Manage) Expectations

We know (usually) what it is we expect from our workplace—which means communicating this before we accept a role is important. If not given the chance, then talking to our managers and being open and up front about what it is we want and expect to help us perform to our best—is important. However, key to this is also **our need to manage our expectations**; and while easier said than done, we must do our part and work with our managers, not against. Managers don't know what they don't know.

Own Your Career

Over 3.6 million U.S. people quit their jobs in April, May, June, and July of 2021 according to the Bureau of Labor Statistics.[7] These stats, which were beginning to edge their way up in 2019, are not just reflective of how people are feeling about their jobs or current situations but are not set to reduce any time soon. In fact, experts suggest stabilization may not occur for two or three more years, as the older of our generation are leading the way on this change.

Trends aside, however, **if the job or workplace is not for you, then move on**. There's no point staying in a career that isn't making you happy. And sure, while consideration might need to be given to timing, the fact that it's an employee's market right now, with unemployment stats at an all-time high, is enough encouragement. And while we are always going to be subjected to societal pressures and predefined ways of living, being, or doing, when it comes to our working lives, our careers, and where we want to be leaving a legacy in the world, we can make decisions and find our pathway to that.

While there are several factors which tie into the challenges surrounding engagement, retention, and recruitment of millennials, there are grounds for reconciliation. And while this might take time, there is remit and certainly scope to incorporate awareness and best practices into workplaces immediately; that of which can mitigate, at the very least, some of the immediate risks and provide support to managers and millennials.

Like all solutions, **key is mutual understanding and respect.** For those workplaces and managers who can understand that part of their role is to help support millennials as they develop their own careers and life pathways, and support their vision and values, will inevitably be rewarded with millennials who give the best of themselves: quality, high-performing talent. For millennials, understanding that the "right" workplaces

[7] U.S. Bureau of Labor Statistics. Economic News Release. 2022. "Job Openings and Labor Turnover Summary." www.bls.gov/news.release/jolts.nr0.htm (accessed October 2022).

offer a place to learn, grow, and evolve is key; and that the "wrong" workplace allows us to become clearer on our wants, encouraging us to take responsibility and control over the workplace we want to be part of, and our careers. And for those workplaces, managers and millennials who can leverage the best from each other—past, present, or future—will be rewarded with lasting experience and the chance to have made a lasting difference.

CHAPTER 6

Millennials in the Workplace

Remote Challenges

The Challenge

While remote working isn't a new concept, and many workplaces were already reaping the benefits and rewards before the pandemic, it's undeniable that this event forced the need to pivot ways of working to the forefront of most, if not all, workplaces.[1] Not least because it became a non-negotiable during periods of lockdown, but because of the outcomes: an ongoing review of corporate life, the traditional values of workplaces, and ways of working. For workplaces, what this move to remote working has offered, is the opportunity for workplaces to understand the deeper values that millennials harbor when it comes to working life—and, in turn, a chance to reimagine new ways of attracting, engaging, and retaining millennial talent, and improving overall performance.

The reflection of flexibility and remote working becoming a "new normal" has been presented through multiple lenses: the uptake and percentage of (white-collar) workers still working remote postpandemic; the reported cases where studies have captured attitudes of workplaces and employees around the success of managing not just the pivot, but the least possible disruption to performance[2]; the Great Resignation highlighting dissatisfaction with old ways of working which by default has forced

---

[1] Global Workplace Analytics. 2022. https://globalworkplaceanalytics.com/tele-commuting-statistics (accessed October 2022).

[2] L. Saad and J.M. Jones. 2021. *Seven in 10 U.S. White-Collar Workers Still Working Remotely*. Gallup, Inc. US. https://news.gallup.com/poll/348743/seven-u.s.-white-collar-workers-still-working-remotely.aspx.

workplaces to rethink operations; and the reception and acceptance of remote integration vis-à-vis the establishment of hybrid models.

However, while many millennials have adapted to this welcome reprieve to a long-standing desire for more flexibility, equality, and accessibility in their working lives, the shift for many workplaces hasn't come without challenges. The mergence to online working and adoption of flexible practices has demanded workplaces to rethink business operations on all levels, and to adjust. Not just to a way of working, such as operations, process, and technology, but more critically, to the management of people.

But beyond the "how to manage remote or hybrid teams effectively" is a more pressing element—attitudinal—of cohorts of millennials who are demanding a change to future ways of working. In fact, studies suggest that not only are **remote ways of working forecasted as both a "trend" and "new normal"** (in some form)[3] but are being increasingly demanded of—including forming new workplaces—from a technologically savvy and values-driven generation who value freedom and autonomy. And with that, a somewhat ultimatum of sorts, which is affecting both retention and recruitment.[4] The need to get this right is a must; which includes the setup, approach, transition, and management of remote millennials.

While studies have found that remote work postpandemic has been a success, to future-proof the sustainability of this model of working, and to ensure its viability (standalone or hybrid), then workplaces need to ensure that the existing challenges and tensions being experienced are being managed.[5] That begins with gaining awareness and control over the current challenges that remote working presents managers. Doing is key to supporting, nurturing, and getting the best out of millennial teams.

[3] Deloitte Insights. 2019. *The Deloitte Global Millennial Survey 2019.*

[4] Live Career. 2021. "Is Remote Work Here to Stay?" www.livecareer.com/resources/careers/planning/is-remote-work-here-to-stay (accessed September 2022).

[5] Price Waterhouse Coopers (PWC). 2021. "It's Time to Reimagine Where and How Work Will Get Done," www.pwc.com/us/en/services/consulting/business-transformation/library/covid-19-us-remote-work-survey.html (accessed September 2022).

The Why

Outside of the pandemic factor that forced remote work onto the global agenda, several key components were already in operation that were slowing moving workplaces to a more modern way of working. Particularly influenced by the increases in technology and arguably evidenced through the rise of startups. However, while many workplaces were already experiencing expansion and scalability "success," what was oftentimes overlooked were the **core foundations to support: structure, process, and people support.** In turn, resulting in several "bumps" in performance, which were further exacerbated by the absence of best practice management.

Consequently, when the pandemic hit, those workplaces that weren't adequately set up equally suffered—bringing to light some critical management issues. And while remote working challenges have been presented around the board generationally, there are several that have been millennial specifics; experienced by, manifested from, resulting in challenges for managers and workplaces. Core to these are communication, workload balance, and mental health—all of which affect performance.

Communication

Communication styles and preferences vary; however, the introduction of remote working places a (solo) emphasis on technology: replacing the in-person meeting with a video call or the "water cooler moment" with an instant messenger "ping." While there are many ways to keep connected and bring remote teams together, the management challenge has been a complex mix of trying to keep engagement high via technology. The inability to gage people's emotions or energy and the absence of visual cues has made it more challenging to connect—and, in turn, presented the need to put extra effort into ways of promoting collaboration. And while one can assume that as a tech-savvy generation, millennials would be au fait with this, the fact is, it hasn't been seamless. For many the constant screen time and endless nature of video calls have produced ill consequences. In fact, studies have shown that the absence of cues, screen fatigue, and technology mishaps, requires the brain to work harder and contributing to fatigue.[6] Leading to a reduction in engaged millennials due to the **exhaustion factor and being "Zoomed out."**

Workload Management

Rising rates of burnout for millennials arguably reflect both an inability to separate work and personal life (boundaries) and an apparent "over worked" situation. The catch-22 of having the flexibility but not being shown how to balance.

Several studies have found that despite the benefits, remote working has presented millennials with a situation of vulnerability: **longer working hours, increased pace and intensity, interference, all contributing to greater stress.**[7]

For many millennials, the feeling of work being "infinite" was (and is) being experienced. While on the one hand, this is beneficial for workplaces that are getting more out of their millennials who are (literally) working around the clock, the reality is, it's contributing to huge amounts of stress and an unbalanced life. Forcing managers to seek solutions and guidance to mitigate the risks of sick leave, low performance, and burnout.

Mental Health

Lack of engagement, underperformance, absences from work: situations which have presented themselves more frequently over the past two years. While the factors on a day to day have already been examined and discussed in Chapter 4, there are several factors which have been compounded by remote work. Specifically, those which have affected mental health. From the undertaking of tasks in isolation, to dependencies on technology, to unbalanced workloads, to personality types (introvert and

---

[6] Robert Half. 2020. "44% of Workers Are Suffering From Video Call Fatigue," www.roberthalf.ca/en/44-of-workers-are-suffering-from-video-call-fatigue-robert-half-research-shows (accessed August 2022).

[7] J. Messenger, L.O. Vargas, L. Gschwind, S. Boehmer, G. Vermeylen, and M. Wilkens. 2017. *Working Anytime, Anywhere: The Effects on the World of Work*, The European Foundation for the Improvement of Living and Working Conditions. https:doi.org/10.2806/425484.

extrovert) and the varying degrees of need for social interaction, to the "always on" effects bleeding into nonwork relationships and social life—it's these factors and nuisances that don't get the attention they need in a remote setting which is impacting mental health. It's these mental health challenges that are becoming increasingly demanding of managers—not just because of the impacts on performance and engagement—but the criticality of finding a way to support.

To understand the challenges more broadly, and get managing remote millennial teams right, there are several factors that need to be considered in parallel; those of which relate to the current and future workforce and workplace demands.

Growing Gig Economy

Remote working aligns with and supports the growing (millennial) Gig Economy—and thus is appealing for talent. It also greatly helps improving the scalability of workplaces. Thanks to the growing Gig Economy, self-employment (and freelancing) is becoming more common as workplaces have come to learn the value in being able to outsource tasks to already trained workers. While workplaces have faced furlough, job cuts, and restructure, the on-hand supply of labor is high; meaning for "get in and get the job done, fast" positions, **a labor market already exists—hungry with millennial talent** waiting for their next opportunity.

From a workforce perceptive, the Gig Economy is a win-win: for workplaces looking to scale existing workforces up and down to meet business demand with less time spent on recruitment processes, and for millennial workers who have a chance to work for multiple workplaces in temporary positions, satisfying the need for diversity and adding value with their expertise.

Workforce Talent

Remote working offers greater access to top millennial talent and an increased diversity of applicants. Offering remote positions means workplaces **attract both a larger pool of candidates and higher-quality candidates** who may not have considered applying for roles due to limitations like geographical location, family commitments, or expenses which no longer exist.

Increases in Productivity

Contrary to perceptions and mistaken beliefs that working from home offers a chance for people to do little or offers more "leisure time" given the absence of the watchful eye of management, these aren't valid. Don't stand up. While historically, older generation managers have typically equated face time in the office with productivity, studies suggest that the average time spent being productive in the office is three to four hours a day.[8] Which means those managers who think they're getting more from millennials because they turn up to the office are mistaken.

To the contrary, several examples exist that show that building high-performing remote teams is possible—and these **productivity benefits** include the ability to work across multiple time zones (24/7), quicker work turnaround times, and improvements in client response times and relationships, to name a few. The increases in productivity also come via increased levels of engagement that can be found with millennial teams. Not just because of the feeling of ownership over their work, and the flexibility afforded to them to balance their lives, but how workplaces that offer this reflect to them: compassionate, open-minded, understanding, and supportive to their needs. And when millennials feel that they are on an equal playing field with their managers, or workplaces, then the commitment they'll provide in return is huge.

Future Workplace

There's no denying that remote working, or the use of hybrid models, is the way of the future for many workplaces. But outside the simple operational aspects to this, what needs to be considered is the planet—specifically

---

[8] Voucher Cloud. 2022. *How Many Productive Hours in a Work Day? Just 2 Hours, 23 Minutes.* www.vouchercloud.com/resources/office-worker-productivity (accessed July 2022).

how the adoption of remote has **supported quality of life and sustainability factors** (e.g., reduction in pollution due to decreases in travel). It's this sustainability component that the millennial workforce wants, and by adopting ways of reducing carbon footprint or emissions via remote working, allows them to do this.

Management Best Practices

What Millennials Want

Even before the pandemic, there were a growing number of millennials feeling the frustrations of working in workplaces that prevented the possibility of working remotely—whether that was the absence of technology to support that, or simply denial. The latter, being fueled by managers claiming all sorts of reasons: the perception it gives, lack of fairness, too costly, too much risk with security, too much work to introduce new policies, it not being "the way we do things," it offers too much of a distraction and won't value add, tax, and legislation issues not allowing it, the "if we make an exception for you, we have to have a blanket rule for everyone which we can't support." Reasons which on face value look valid, but unless evidence-based, have a hard time standing up—especially for millennials who will challenge this by asking "why," and if a problem, will likely come back with a solution. In situations where millennials find themselves with managers who continue to articulate "no," find themselves at a loss—frustrated even—with the limitation to their desires. And for this generation, it speaks volumes in terms of both who that manager (or workplace) is and how they feel about their millennials: rigid, inflexible, self-centered, untrusting, and uncompassionate. Situations like this are more than just the "no"—and from an engagement and retention perspective, are the most problematic. Millennials can read through the lines.

While many workplaces are either establishing or adjusting to the future office postpandemic, there's no denying that for many millennials, they will no longer be choosing workplaces where a remote way of working option—at least on occasion—isn't offered (industry-specific, of course). **Millennials value being given the reins of control over their**

lives—and with work-life integration and flexibility as core principles, it makes sense. Fortunately, there are a great deal of workplaces that have recognized the golden opportunity that offering this brings vis-à-vis quality talent and enhanced productivity.

With remote or hybrid becoming the dominant way of working, managers and workplaces need to adjust not only to the practicalities of working in a new way but also a shift in attitudes, beliefs, and the adoption of a new perspective that focus more on the benefits and how this supports millennial teams, versus any resistance to change or a focus on problems.

Outside of addressing the problems that remote work presents, to be effective in their jobs, there are key things that millennials want, and need, from their managers. And while these needs can be considered "general," they are even more pertinent in the remote setting—and for good reason.

Trust

Millennials **need managers to trust them to do their work.** Trust is one of the biggest challenges that managers express when it comes to managing remote teams. If millennials don't feel trusted or are in a situation where managers are constantly checking in and they have no breathing room to get on and do what they need to, then it becomes suffocating, stressful, and demotivating. And with an already aversion to micro-managing ways, it won't serve them or you well. Building trust takes time, but it's well worth the investment. Trust them to deliver.

Flexibility

Millennials **need managers who appreciate the need for flexibility**— which includes times they may choose to come into the hybrid office, what hours they may need to work, and what and how to prioritize. Managers must remember that even outside of the work-life integration values, they are often doing several things: working on other projects, studying, second jobs, families, social, and sports. And while they'll always be respectful of the traditional "8-hour workday" (even if they prefer their outputs to be judged on merit and effort versus how long they spend in front of their screen), the ability to be able to complete this "8 hours" around their other commitments is important.

Respect

Millennials **need managers to treat them with respect**. That being both their workloads and their other priorities—but most importantly, being respected as an adult. With the age span of millennials being between 25 and 40, there is variation for how other older colleagues may perceive them. Irrespective, 25 years or 40, both want to be treated like an adult—which includes being able to manage their own workload and time without feeling any guilt or having to prove self or what was being worked on, when.

Support

This is perhaps one of the most critical things millennials want—and it's multifaceted—in fact, arguably wholistic. This support is about setting them up for success in a remote way, and in some parts recognizing that while there's ease, remote working offers a different set of challenges that need to be accounted for. Key for managers is recognizing those challenges and **working with millennials to work out support, systems, or frameworks** to make both the adjustment and continuation of this way of working both feasible and a viable long-term option for them.

How to Support

Mastering remote working is about finding the right strategies. Remote work becomes more efficient when expectations are set for the way things are done. Having a clear structure and strategies in place will help millennials feel supported and continue to perform.

Communication

Consider communication needs. Communication has always been a top issue for remote working teams. It isn't just about the style of communication and the need to consider the variation of generations, but the challenge of getting information in a timely way. It often feels more laborious trying to get some things done, particularly when it involves other people. (And people you can't see in real life.)

Generally, best practice would see **multiple forms of communication modes being offered** to accommodate styles. However, when it comes to remote—selecting and sticking with one platform (e.g., Teams or Slack) is going to be the most conducive for smooth communications. And particularly for millennials who are digital natives, adopting and using technology to get things done is key.

Provide opportunities for social interaction. Research already points to the reality that millennials struggle most with feelings of loneliness and isolation. Working remote can exacerbate that—and trying to develop or maintain feelings of connectedness with our co-workers via technology can be challenging. One way to mitigate this is to **find ways for millennials to interact socially in person.** And while this might not be feasible for all types of workplaces frequently, a once or twice-a-year human interaction or event should be encouraged. Humans are social creatures after all—and millennials who are navigated toward teams and collaboration would strongly benefit.

Maintaining company culture. Creating and maintaining a positive company culture can be challenging for workplaces—add in the remote element, and it becomes even harder. Engaging and motivating remote teams takes more effort and consideration. That said there are many ways to use technology to make the best of meetings and virtual gatherings where teams can enjoy their time together, and harmonious cultures and relationships can be nourished.

Workload Management

Establish structure and set expectations. Lack of face-to-face supervision is one of the most common concerns expressed by managers and employees. Managers have expressed concerns that employees will not work as hard, while employees struggle with reduced communication and access to managerial support. **Millennials want and require structure** (this isn't to be confused with micro-management).

Providing a structure, or plan, helps to resolve some of these issues. It is also particularly important for millennials (and Gen Z) who may lack initiative or the ability to self-manage. Don't always assume that what you say is understood by your millennials: have them relay back to you what you've asked, including when tasks are due. This will mitigate delays, or tasks not being completed correctly (or at all). This structure could start with daily check-ins with employees; a one-on-one call is one of the most successful ways of doing this. Or planning out daily or weekly tasks, which is especially helpful to employees who require a more "hands on" approach.

Help set boundaries. Remote working requires discipline, especially when it comes to time management of tasks, workload, and the minimization of distractions. And while millennials are generally able to get on with things well, given their focus and initiative, they would benefit from support. **Help them set boundaries,** which includes support in prioritizing their workloads through a schedule that prevents overworking and encourages them to switch off outside of work for their personal lives.

Review performance measures. Whether it's reviewing general Key performance indicators (KPIs), or having "softer" ways of measuring performance, having **something tangible that can be worked toward** will help instill confidence both in your millennial teams (by giving them purpose or goals) and managers. These measurable, however, should be realistic and achievable—and checked against the tangibility of achievability given the extra effort that may be required. Simply because the working environment has changed, doesn't mean that performance measures should be out of reach.

Consider the set up. A consideration for managers and millennials is ergonomics and environment. While some may not have considered this Occupational Health and Safety topic, the reality is **the environment we're working in makes a difference.** "How" people are working remotely, and their home office arrangements, have a huge impact on productivity, health, well-being, and motivation. Managing workloads should also include the practicalities or where the work is being undertaken.

Mental Health

Offer encouragement and emotional support. The transition from office to working from home takes time and isn't always easy. It is important for managers to **acknowledge stress, anxieties, and concerns** of their millennials and provide emotional support. Where possible, workplaces should be investing in mental health, diversity, and inclusion initiatives or connecting with relevant support networks to ensure employees are supported.

Accept that adjustment takes time. Managers often express feeling uncomfortable or feeling like they have a lack of control; feelings which take time to move through because of the adjustment to change. These feelings—the **establishment of trust and managing through change**—are a two-way street. Which means it's likely there will be millennials feeling the same. Accepting and acknowledging are key to offering compassion—both to yourself and others.

For Millennials: How to Get What You Want

Controversial or not, the pandemic did millennials a huge favor: It redefined the workplace, and for those of us who had been longing for more flexibility, it brought that. For those in our generation already working that way, safe to say that things for you may not have changed too drastically—with the expectation (perhaps) of letting go of any subconscious guilt because you've already been enjoying the fruits of labor working this way, while friends and colleagues were none the wiser in their workplaces.

Jokes and speculation aside, with the "having of our cake" of remote or hybrid options, we must make sure we're playing our part to ensure that we're doing the best we can, for ourselves and our workplace. While workplaces have put a lot of effort into changing ways of working and coming up to speed, we know that everything is about co-creation. With that, **we need to support our managers and workplaces as they transition** to new or determine how best to support their workforce in the best way possible.

The top challenges that managers are facing, we too are experiencing. Communication and feeling connected through technology, managing our workloads, and mental health—all of which affect keeping us motivated and engaged and, in turn, performing to the best we can." Remote work has **reallocated a large part of the responsibility of how we work back to us**—whether we know it or not. Managing ourselves is key. Prioritizing our work, setting boundaries, and being better communicators are all critical for us to succeed in our remote work lives.

Communication

Managing remotely is harder. For us, acknowledging this is important. And while there's no "expectation" set by our managers, it's probably safe to say they would appreciate being met halfway. We are a cohort of people who are comfortable and familiar with technology, including the benefits and how we feel when we're given the opportunity to have the freedom we desire. This makes us great teachers for our managers—and opens a door to a collaborative way of working, which builds trust. Demonstrating understanding (or appreciation), removing any unhelpful expectations, and **being more willing to support managers as they support you** is highly likely going to result in better working conditions for you.

Workload Management

At the risk of sounding like I'm teaching you to suck eggs, sometimes it's easier to back to basics: set up a schedule and prioritize the things in your day. Famous author, speaker, and radio broadcaster Earl Nightingale once said, "No one manages time. Time cannot be managed. We can manage activities." Which means key for us in managing out workload is to make it manageable. With the best intents, **we can overcommit ourselves,** and as much as we like to see our list of accomplishments crossed off or the virtual unicorn dancing across the computer screen, being realistic is key. If needed, **work with your manager to set up a plan** with priorities and due dates to make your workload lighter and more manageable.

Mental Health

It's easy to slip into overworking—and we can be sticklers for it—which is why we must be even more aware of the habits that may have become developed. While our managers are one part of the mental health equation, we also need to take control. We know (we feel it) when things are a little unbalanced. Speaking up when we're feeling pressured, going into the office for human connection, saying "no," and taking time out when we need are all ways of protecting our own well-being.

From an isolation and loneliness perspective, this also takes effort—and in some parts, courage. Including social breaks with friends or family, working from a co-working space or office on occasion, or even going to your local café and ways to get the "human fix"—and one that we can manage our tolerance around. Cabin fever happens, and for those of us who are more digital nomadic in nature, understand the complexities when relationships are constantly virtual.

Performance

Finally is our performance and those things that keep us engaged. Let's face it, being at home or on a working holiday does make it harder to keep focused—not least because of the interruptions and distractions. However, we also know that we can be the most productive when not in the office—because of the same reasons in avoiding the interruptions and distractions of an office. This is where our goals come into play: and they should be strong enough to want to keep motivating us to do what we need to do, despite the external conditions. If you don't have goals, or KPIs that you have been actively part of developing, then find them. While we are self-starters and can manage ourselves, **we need to ensure that our performance is sustainable**—and continues to build trust in our managers that we are maintaining our work ethic, even if not under direct physical supervision.

While the pandemic presented many workplaces with the challenge of navigating unchartered waters with remote working, including the "how to manage" a remote workforce, there have been several silver linings. For millennials, a far greater need to manage themselves—including the things that matter; allowing space for needs identification and greater control over work-life management. For workplaces, an opportunity to understand how millennials prefer to work; adopting a new approach and transition to support the current and future workforce. One that will enhance engagement, retention, and business performance if maintained.

Closing Note

The Future Is Now

The landscape of workplaces is undoubtedly changing and will continue to change. While the future workplace and careers will continue to evolve, including future skills needed to thrive in the new and improved environments, at the heart of these changes—and those who will be fundamental to navigating a changing world—are leaders. Those leaders—current and future—are millennials.

There are factors and trends that we do know.[1] That **population aging** will change the workforce: on the one hand, the demographic trends that currently present a multigenerational workforce will shift as Baby Boomers retire and younger generations—especially Gen Z—move into the workforce; on the other, the extension of life longevity may impact retirement age—confounded by global impacts such as rising cost of living and, in turn, potentially affecting the labor market vis-à-vis shortages of jobs. **New technologies** will continue to shape the future of work: changes in work-life patterns, habits, collaboration, innovative ways of working, and more flexibility—have all been accelerated by technology and globalization. This also includes the type of work—including an increase in temporary and other diverse forms of work that offer more frequency in job switching and the ability to use the technology in a more enhanced way. The **skills required for future work** will need to adapt to the needs of the planet, and there be greater emphasis on education providers and employers working collaboratively together.

But trends and statistics aside, what does this mean, and how does this affect our future workforce and millennial leaders?

---

[1] *Promoting an Age-Inclusive Workforce: Living, Learning and Earning Longer.* 2020. Organization for Economic Cooperation and Development (OECD). https://doi.org/10.1787/59752153-en.

The future of work is going to depend as much on the leader as it is the type of career or skills that are identified, or that which employees bring to the table. It's for this reason that getting millennials up and running into positions of power and leveraging the skills, values, and experience they bring—including a strong focus and emphasis on equality, diversity, and inclusion, factors that support an integrated and more harmonious culture and ways of working—is critical.

The future workplace will be dependent on solid leadership that is sitting—sits at—the heart of all workplaces. For those leaders (Boomers) who have outgrown the current environment, there needs to be a willingness to move aside and let rejuvenated energy into the space. Because the future workplace will be one of innovation, excitement, and productivity as we allow the ideas of the emerging workforce to take the seat and drive sustainable changes that we are—and have been—needing for such a long time.

We live in a diverse world; there's no denying that this presents both challenges and beauty. As we move toward the future, we must give those leaders who are able and willing to work toward a brighter more collaborative future—one where needs and wants are met, differences and contrast are accepted and appreciated, and approaches to focusing on the greater good of people and the planet exist—the space to act.

For current managers, it's your job to ensure that those sitting at the table right now—those in the drivers' seat—are educated and provided with the support needed to take them to the next level of leadership expansion. Let them flourish; create the space for them to stand up, take ownership, and illustrate their power and drive—the very things they were born to do.

For current leaders—for those preparing and managing the current workforce who are needing to identify the best skills to get people ready into the positions of power, we tell you this: those skills needed will be more of the same—what exists but aren't leveraged, and therefore done in a different way.

Communication is critical, and leaders must be teaching younger generations to speak more fluently in the day to day. Technology is only one way, and with the diverse platforms that this world will continue to see evolve and come into play, the future leaders need to be ready to adapt the languages that suit the diverse audiences that will be presented.

Problem solving and the ability to "fix things" are core traits of millennials, we know that. However, to truly tap into this, they need to be given permission—to be both given the problem and the ability to work out the solution, building both their capability and confidence in their abilities. For some managers (who know who you are), this will require you to step out of the protection mode and let your millennials fall and fail and get back up so they can do it, again and again, to facilitate their growth—benefitting not just themselves but the company.

Resilience is critical, not just for their own well-being—as mental health is a challenge—but for the future of the world. The more resilient millennials are, the less likely they are to tolerate any of the "noise" that is seen around the world. More authenticity and speaking of truth, more transparency and openness, more humility, and less hostility. All those soft skills—complemented by the values and traits that already sit at the core—are accessible, but only if they are given the platform to express that.

We know that there is uncertainly with what the world might look like. Fear exists among many: for leaders and executives all around the world about what and how to manage changing workforces and the nature of work; for millennials and Gen Z about what the future of work may look like, including their own ability to find careers and jobs that are meaningful.

But the essence of leadership—and that which lies at the heart of millennials—will be those fundamental skills and values that they already harbor; the essence of who they are and what they exist for. It's this—them—who is going to bring this world into the next level of beingness and drive humanity—which includes the future of our workforce—to a greater level of awareness and consciousness on a global scale. **Because the future is in the hands of millennials—and that future, is now.**

Resources

The following templates have been designed to support managers. These tables may be used to assess the current workplace environment and management practices against key areas of importance relevant to millennials. These templates are not exclusive but are intended to act as a guide.

Chapter 1 Being Millennial: Values, Traits, and Skills

Identified area (millennial need)	Current state assessment	Future state actions	Review date	Outcomes
Supportive environment				
Celebrating individuality				
Safe space for conversations				
Flexibility in when, where, and how work is done				
Ability to lead, invoke change and innovation				
Encouraging autonomy and creative freedom				
Use of technology to bring about efficiencies				
Development of goals				

Chapter 2 *The Millennial World: Top Challenges and Impacts to Workplaces*

Identified area (millennial need)	Current state assessment	Future state actions	Review date	Outcomes
"Financial fit"—consider financial situation (assess needs, options for flexibility or incentives)				
"Employment fit"—flexibility in ways of working, inclusive culture (understand values, ambitions)				
"Education fit"—viable career pathway and options for learning and development (identify wants, nurture talent)				
"Mental health fit"—strategies to support (attitude, prioritization, emotional support, systems)				

Chapter 3 *Millennials in the Workplace: Careers and Expectations*

Identified area (millennial need)	Current state assessment	Future state actions	Review date	Outcomes
Identification of individual needs (have the right questions been asked)				
Expectation setting (have these been done in a meaningful way)				
Permission to fail (supporting discovery, encouraging decision making)				
Identification of motivators (external and intrinsic)				
Consideration to future skills and careers				

Chapter 4 *Millennials in the Workplace: Generational Diversity and Management*

Identified area (millennial need)	Current state assessment	Future state actions	Review date	Outcomes
Managers are leadership-oriented, open-minded, similar/shared values				
Identification of individual "why" has occurred				
Provide consistent feedback				
Focus on team building and community				
Reverse mentoring considered/adopted				

Chapter 5 Millennials in the Workplace: Engage, Retain, Recruit

Identified area (millennial need)	Current state assessment	Future state actions	Review date	Outcomes
Culture of well-being (leadership, values, beliefs, attitudes, and set of behaviors)				
Culture of trust (made an explicit objective)				
Promotes and fosters a sense of belonging				
Promotes collaboration and "at level" thinking				
Promotes diversity and inclusivity				
Supports sustainability, social/global responsibility, and impact				
Supports decision making and solid leadership				
Defined vision, mission, and values				

Chapter 6 Millennials in the Workplace: Remote Challenges

Identified area (millennial need)	Current state assessment	Future state actions	Review date	Outcomes
Demonstrating trust for teams				
Communication needs, styles, and preferences considered				
Opportunities for social interaction				
Using technology to support positive culture				
Providing structure and plan				
Supporting boundary setting (start and end work times) and workload management				
Identification of performance goals or KPIs				
Ergonomic assessment				
Emotional support and mental health considerations				

References

"Are We Trained for Work? Employee and Practitioner Perspectives on UK L&D." 2022. www.digits.co.uk/are-we-trained-for-work-confirmation/ (accessed October 2022).

Bensinger, DuPont & Associates. 2015. *Anxiety and Work: The Impact of Anxiety on Different Generations of Employees*. https://us.morneaushepell.com/.

Bureau of Labor Statistics. 2020. cited in *The Truth About Millennial Turnover*. Recruiting.com, US. www.recruiting.com/blog/the-truth-about-millennial-turnover/.

Carnegie, D. 2018. *Managers Matter: A Relationship-Centered Approach to Engagement*. www.dalecarnegie.com.

Curran, T. and A.P. Hill. 2017. "Perfectionism Is Increasing Over Time: A Meta-Analysis of Birth Cohort Differences From 1989 to 2016." *Psychological Bulletin*.

Curran. T. and P.H. Andrew. 2019. "Perfectionism Is Increasing Over Time: A Meta-Analysis of Birth Cohort Differences From 1989 to 2016." *Psychological Bulletin* 145, no. 4, pp. 410–429.

Deloitte Insights. 2019. *The Deloitte Global Millennial Survey 2019*.

Deloitte Insights. 2022. *The Deloitte Global 2022 Gen Z and Millennial Survey*.

Federal Reserve Bank. 2017. "Changes in U.S. Family Finances From 2013 to 2016: Evidence From the Survey of Consumer Finances." *Federal Reserve Bulletin* 103, no. 3, pp. 1–42.

Foster, T. 2017. *Multigenerational Impacts on the Workplace*. Gloria Cordes Larson Center for Women and Business (CWB). Bentley University.

Global Workplace Analytics. 2022. https://globalworkplaceanalytics.com/tele commuting-statistics (accessed September 2022).

Goodhire. 2022. *Horrible Bosses: Are American Workers Quitting Their Jobs or Quitting Their Managers?*. www.goodhire.com/resources/articles/horrible-bosses-survey/.

Gruttadaro, D. and D. Crudo. 2012. *College Students Speak: A Survey Report on Mental Health*. U.S.: The National Alliance on Mental Illness.

Henriques, G. 2014. "The College Student Mental Health Crisis Today's College Students Are Suffering From an Epidemic of Mental Illnesses." *Psychology Today*. www.psychologytoday.com.

How Millennials Want to Work and Live. 2016. U.S.: Gallup Inc. www.gallup .com/workplace/238073/millennials-work-live.

How Millennials Want to Work and Live. 2018. U.S.: Gallup, Inc. www.gallup .com/workplace/238073/millennials-work-live.aspx.

Hulten, C.R. and V.A. Ramey. 2018. *Education, Skills, and Technical Change: Implications for Future US GDP Growth.* University of Chicago Press. www .nber.org/books/hult-12.

IBM Study. 2015. *The Real Story Behind Millennials in the Workplace.* www .multivu.com/players/English/7428151-ibm-millennials-workplace-myths/.

Kahn, L.B. 2010. "The Long-Term Labor Market Consequences of Graduating From College in a Bad Economy." *Labour Economics* 17, no. 2, pp. 303–316. https://doi.org/10.1016/j.labeco.2009.09.002.

Kingman. D. 2018. *New IF Research Sows That Young Adults' Wellbeing Has Fallen by 10% Since Mid-1990s.* Intergenerational Foundation. www.if.org.uk/.

Knight, J.R., H. Weschler, M. Kuo, M. Seibring, E.R. Weitzman, and M.A. Schuckit. 2015. "Alcohol Abuse and Dependence Among U.S. College Students." *Journal of Studies on Alcohol* 63, no. 3, pp. 263–270.

Live Career. 2021. "Is Remote Work Here to Stay?" www.livecareer.com/ resources/careers/planning/is-remote-work-here-to-stay (accessed September 2022).

McCreary, M. 2015. *Anxiety and Work: The Impact of Anxiety on Different Generations of Employees.* U.S.: Morneau Shepell.

Messenger, J., O. Vargas Llave, L. Gschwind, S. Boehmer, G. Vermeylen, and M. Wilkens. 2017. *Working Anytime, Anywhere: The Effects on the World of Work.* The European Foundation for the Improvement of Living and Working Conditions. https://doi:10.2806/425484.

Ngotngamwong, R. 2020. *A Study of Millennial Job Satisfaction and Retention* 21, pp. 47–58.

Phillips C. and J. Hopelain. 2015. *What Do Millennials Want in a Job? Insights for Making Talent Brands Millennial-Relevant.* Brand Amplitude, LLC.

Price Waterhouse Coopers (PWC). 2021. "It's Time to Reimagine Where and How Work Will Get Done." www.pwc.com/us/en/services/consulting/ business-transformation/library/covid-19-us-remote-work-survey.html (accessed September 2022).

Price Waterhouse Coopers (PWC). 2022. *Workforce of the Futures. The Competing Forces Shaping 2030.*" https://pwc.to/2Rfozuq.

Robert Half. 2020. "44% of Workers Are Suffering From Video Call Fatigue." www.roberthalf.ca/en/44-of-workers-are-suffering-from-video-call-fatigue-robert-half-research-shows (accessed August 2022).

Robert Walters Whitepaper. 2022. *Attracting and Retaining Millennial Professionals.* www.robertwalters.com.

Saad, L. and J.M. Jones. 2021. *Seven in 10 U.S. White-Collar Workers Still Working Remotely.* U.S.: Gallup, Inc. https://news.gallup.com/poll/348743/ seven-u.s.-white-collar-workers-still-working-remotely.aspx.

Society for Human Resource Management. 2020. cited in *Survey: 84 Percent of U.S. Workers Blame Bad Managers for Creating Unnecessary Stress.* www.shrm.org/about-shrm/press-room/press-releases/pages/survey-84-percent-of-us-workers-blame-bad-managers-for-creating-unnecessary-stress-.aspx.

Statistics and Research on Eating Disorders. 2018. The National Eating Disorders Association. www.nationaleatingdisorders.org.

U.S. Bureau of Labor Statistics. Economic News Release. 2022. "Job Openings and Labor Turnover Summary." www.bls.gov/news.release/jolts.nr0.htm (accessed October 2022).

United Nations, Department of Economic and Social Affairs, Population Division. 2019. *World Population Prospects 2019: Highlights* (ST/ESA/SER.A/423).

Voucher Cloud. 2022. *How Many Productive Hours in a Work Day? Just 2 Hours, 23 Minutes...* www.vouchercloud.com/resources/office-worker-productivity (accessed July 2022).

Workjam. 2022. *Millennials Far More Likely to Quit Jobs Than Gen Z, Bosses Say.* www.workjam.com/newsroom/bloomberg-millennials-far-more-likely-to-quit-jobs-than-gen-z/.

About the Author

Jacqueline Cripps is a consultant, writer, and speaker with a background in social sciences and psychology. Her niche expertise lies in helping workplaces understand the millennial generation. She is passionate about creating awareness, educating others, and bringing about positive change. Jacqueline writes for numerous publications, is the author of two other nonfiction books, and has an extensive media portfolio. As a creative and avid traveler, Jacqueline spends her time between London and New York.

Index